ESSAYS IN INTERNATIONAL ECONOMICS

No. 222, June 2001

THE JAPANESE BANKING CRISIS OF THE 1990s: SOURCES AND LESSONS

AKIHIRO KANAYA

AND

DAVID WOO

INTERNATIONAL ECONOMICS SECTION

DEPARTMENT OF ECONOMICS
PRINCETON UNIVERSITY
PRINCETON, NEW JERSEY

INTERNATIONAL ECONOMICS SECTION
EDITORIAL STAFF

Gene M. Grossman *Director*

Pierre-Olivier Gourinchas *Assistant Director*

Margaret B. Riccardi, *Editor*

Sharon B. Ernst, *Editorial Aide*

Lalitha H. Chandra, *Subscriptions and Orders*

Library of Congress Cataloging-in-Publication Data

Kanaya, Akihiro.
    The Japanese banking crisis of the 1990s: sources and lessons / Akihiro Kanaya and David Woo.
    p. cm. — (Essays in international economics, ISSN 0071-142X; no. 222)
    Includes bibliographical references.
    ISBN 0-88165-129-X
    1. Banks and banking—Japan.   2. Banks and banking—Deregulation—Japan   3. Corporate governance—Japan   I. Woo, David.   II. Title.   III. Series: Essays in international economics.
    (Princeton, N.J.); no. 222.
    HG136.P7 no. 222 [HG3324]   2001024832
    332'.042s—dc21 [332.1'0952'090]   CIP

Printed in the United States of America by Princeton University Printing Services at Princeton, New Jersey

International Standard Serial Number: 0071-142X
International Standard Book Number: 0-88165-129-X
Library of Congress Catalog Card Number: 2001024832

International Economics Section
  Department of Economics, Fisher Hall
  Princeton University
  Princeton, New Jersey 08544-1021

Tel: 609-258-4048
Fax: 609-258-1374
E-mail: ies@princeton.edu
Url: www.princeton.edu/~ies

CONTENTS

TABLES

BOX

FIGURES

THE JAPANESE BANKING CRISIS OF THE 1990S: SOURCES AND LESSONS

1 Introduction

For much of the past decade, Japan has witnessed a steady decline in the health of its banking system. This deterioration, which began with the bursting of the asset bubble at the end of the 1980s, culminated in a full-blown systemic crisis in 1997 following the failure of several high-profile financial institutions. Given the relatively large size of Japanese banks and their predominance in corporate funding in Japan, this crisis has had profound implications for both the Japanese and global economies.

A study of the Japanese banking crisis is useful for three reasons. First, most of its underlying causes—excessive asset expansion during periods of economic boom, liberalization without an appropriate adjustment to the regulatory environment, weak corporate governance and regulatory forbearance when the system is under stress—are typical of banking crises in general. Second, the Japanese banking crisis serves as a warning that such problems may befall seemingly robust and relatively sophisticated financial systems; the fact that only a decade ago, Japanese banks were considered to be among the strongest in the world makes the extent of their decline all the more remarkable (Table 1). Third, the Japanese experience demonstrates that the costs to the economy of a banking crisis can be considerable. In addition to the fiscal cost of restructuring the banks (government funds equivalent to about 12 percent of gross domestic product [GDP] have already been allocated), the banking crisis has probably been largely responsible for the stagnation of the Japanese economy during the 1990s (Brunner and Kamin, 1998; Bayoumi, 1999; Motonishi and Yoshikawa, 1999).[1]

The authors wrote this essay while they were both at the Monetary and Exchange Affairs Department at the International Monetary Fund. They are grateful to Akira Ariyoshi, Tamin Bayoumi, Christian Beddies, Charles Collyns, Charles Enoch, Peter Hayward, Richard Katz, Patricia Hagan Kuwayama, Marina Moretti, Elizabeth Milne, James Morsink, Hugh Patrick, Toshitaka Sekine, and David Weinstein for their helpful comments, and to Margalit Shinar for her editorial assistance.

[1] The weakening of the banks is likely to have reduced the effectiveness of loose monetary policies in stimulating the economy (Morsink and Bayoumi, 1999; Sekine, 1999; Woo, 1999).

TABLE 1

CREDIT RATINGS OF JAPANESE CITY BANKS

	Bank of Tokyo-Mitsubishi	Dai-Ichi Kangyo Bank	Fuji Bank	Sakura Bank	Sanwa Bank	Sumitomo Bank	Tokai Bank
1980	—	B	A/B	—	B	A/B	B
1981	—	B	A/B	—	B	A/B	B
1982	—	B/C	A/B	—	B	A/B	B
1983	—	B/C	A/B	—	B	A/B	B
1984	—	B	B	—	A/B	A/B	B
1985	—	B	B	—	A/B	A/B	B/C
1986	—	B	B	—	B	B	B/C
1987	—	B	B	—	B	B	C
1988	—	B	B	—	B	B	B/C
1989	—	B	B	—	B	B	B/C
1990	—	B	B	B/C	B	B	B/C
1991	—	B	B	B/C	B	B	B/C
1992	—	B/C	B/C	B/C	B/C	B/C	B/C
1993	—	B/C	B/C	C	B/C	B/C	B/C
1994	—	B/C	B/C	C	B/C	B/C	B/C
1995	—	B/C	C	C/D	B/C	B/C	C
1996	B/C	C	C	D	C	C	C/D
1997	B/C	C	C/D	D	C	C	C/D
1998	C	D	D	D	C/D	C/D	D
1999	C/D	D	D	D	D	C/D	D

SOURCE: Fitch IBCA.

This essay examines the Japanese banking system during the 1990s in order to understand what exactly went wrong and why it has been taking so long for the system to recover. The essay covers about fifteen years, beginning with the last years of the bubble and ending with several recent positive developments. It traces the roots of the problems in the banking system to an acceleration in deregulation and a deepening of the capital markets in the late 1980s, which exacerbated the problem of overcapacity in the system. The banks were further weakened by the absence of risk-management controls and of an adequate regulatory and supervisory framework, the lack of which allowed for heightened competition and risk taking. This survey will argue that the subsequent "gamble for resurrection" prompted a relaxation of credit conditions for most of the 1990s.

A unique characteristic of the Japanese banking crisis is its exceptionally long duration compared to similar crises elsewhere in the world (Hutchison and McDill, 1999; Nishimura, 1999). Weak corporate governance in Japan and regulatory forbearance stifled any incentive for meaningful restructuring of banks and their corporate borrowers. These two factors, by contributing to what might have been an unnecessary prolongation of the crisis, inevitably raised the cost of the final resolution.

Attempts to understand the Japanese banking crisis better have given rise to a number of recent surveys. Cargill, Hutchison, and Ito (1997), for example, provide a chronological overview of the major events and argue that moral hazard associated with the deposit-insurance scheme was a leading factor behind the further deterioration of weak banks. Hoshi and Kashyap (1999) cover the impact of deregulation on the banking system and offer some quantification of its likely future shrinkage. Corbett (2000a) documents and analyzes the policy response to the crisis. Hutchison and McDill (1999) and Corbett (2000b) cast the Japanese banking crisis in international perspective. Cargill (2000) identifies five causes relating chiefly to the inadequacy of the supervisory and resolution framework. The present essay draws from this growing literature and adds to it by providing more details about the interaction between bank behavior and the regulatory, tax, accounting, and legal frameworks. The discussion also gives more prominence to the role of corporate governance than previous surveys have given and brings to light further evidence of regulatory forbearance.

The essay is structured as follows. Section 2 reviews the background to the asset-bubble economy and the effects of the bubble's collapse on the banking system. Section 3 describes the regulatory framework, including the introduction of the Basle Capital Standard and the existing loan classification and loan-loss provisioning practices. Section 4 examines the responses of banks to the new banking environment. Sections 5 and 6 discuss the issue of bank corporate governance and the environment prior to the banking crisis. Section 7 reviews the resolution strategy, including the legal resolution framework and the recapitalization of the banks by the government. Section 8 identifies some recent positive developments. Section 9 concludes the discussion.

2   The Bubble Economy

Preconditions

During the second half of the 1980s, the Japanese macroeconomic environment was characterized by above-trend economic growth and near-zero inflation. These positive conditions, resulting in a significant decline in the country risk premium and a marked upward adjustment in growth expectations, boosted asset prices and fueled rapid credit expansion (Yamaguchi, 1999). The same period also witnessed an acceleration in the pace of financial liberalization and deregulation, which consisted of:

• the relaxation of interest-rate controls,[2] starting with the liberalization of term deposit rates in 1985 (Box 1);

• the deregulation of capital markets, including the lifting, in 1984, of the prohibition on short-term euro-yen loans to domestic borrowers (loans that are not subject to interest-rate controls); the gradual removal of restrictions on access to the corporate bond market;[3] and the creation of the commercial-paper market in 1987. The last two developments significantly strengthened the ability of large corporations to borrow directly from the market;

• the relaxation of restrictions on permissible activities of previously tightly segregated institutions, including the raising of different types of lending ceilings. For example, the agricultural, fishery, and credit cooperatives saw an increase in their lending ceilings to nonmembers.

These developments had important consequences for banks and other depository institutions (Hoshi and Kashyap, 1999). The incipient price competition that was beginning to place downward pressure on banks' risk-adjusted interest-rate margins led them to expand the riskier segments of their loan portfolios.[4] In particular, they sharply increased their lending to consumers, to the real estate industry, and to small and medium-sized enterprises (Table 2). Meanwhile, their persistent focus on market share,[5] and the fact that their lending decisions

---

[2] This was partly in response to pressure from the U.S. government, which took the position that liberalization of the financial system in Japan would help address the strong dollar problem by stimulating demand for yen-denominated instruments and would help U.S. financial institutions break into the Japanese market.

[3] By the late 1980s, rated firms were able to avoid meeting the criteria set by the Bond Issuance Committee. All rules relating to bond issues were abolished in 1996.

[4] Marsh and Paul (1996) argue that profit margins of Japanese banks, in decline since the early 1970s, were temporarily boosted in the late 1980s by a shift toward higher risk loans.

[5] The preoccupation of banks with market share is in many ways a vestige of the regime of interest-rate control. Under that regime, the fact that banks' lending spreads were more or less fixed and that they derived most of their income from their interest earnings meant that their outstanding loans largely determined the size of their net income. Noma (1986) has shown, moreover, that Japanese banks are more interested in expanding their scales of operations than in maximizing profits.

4

BOX 1
DEREGULATION OF INTEREST RATES IN JAPAN

Interest-Rate Controls

The Temporary Interest Rate Adjustment Law (TIRAL), introduced in 1947, provided the principal framework for interest-rate control in Japan. It allowed the Ministry of Finance to convene the Policy Board of the Bank of Japan in order to establish, revise, or abolish interest-rate ceilings for financial institutions. The Policy Board set the ceilings in consultation with the Interest Adjustment Council (comprising representatives from industry, the Ministry of Finance, and the Bank of Japan). The TIRAL allowed the Bank of Japan to develop detailed guidelines for ceilings on deposit rates (time deposits, fixed savings, installment savings, current deposits, deposits for tax payment, ordinary deposits, special deposits) and on short-term lending rates, as well as on rates of discounted bills the sum of which was greater than one million yen and the maturity of which was less than one year. The TIRAL applied to city banks, regional banks, trust banks, long-term credit banks, *shinkin* banks,° the Norinchukin Bank, the Shoko Chukin Bank, credit cooperatives, labor banks, and agricultural cooperatives. The *shinkin* banks, and the agricultural and credit cooperatives were, however, exempt from regulations on lending rates. Government financial institutions and postal savings were also exempt from the TIRAL.

As the result of interest-rate control, there was very little interest-rate variation among different financial institutions. Following the loosening of controls on lending rates in 1959, the Federation of Bankers Association of Japan introduced a system that set short-term lending rates between the official discount rate and the ceiling imposed by the TIRAL. This system was abolished in April 1974 when the Antimonopoly Law was tightened. In practice, however, the bank at which the chairman of the Federation of Bankers served would announce its rates of interest and the other banks would follow suit. For long-term lending rates, there were no formal restrictions. However, the long-term prime rates charged to electric power and other blue-chip companies by long-term credit banks, trust banks, and insurance companies were made public and functioned as the basis for other rates. These rates rarely varied by lending institution.

Deregulation

In 1979, certificates of deposit (CDs) were introduced as deposits exempt from the TIRAL. When they were first introduced, their issues were required to be of the minimum size of 500 million yen and of between one to six months' maturity. Following the recommendation of the Japan-U.S. Yen-Dollar Ad Hoc Committee in May 1984, deregulation of deposit rates accelerated, starting with large deposits. In March 1985, term deposits with market interest rates were introduced. Although they were not exempt from the TIRAL, their rate ceilings were high enough for banks to peg the rates to the CD rates. In October 1988, large deposits (initially restricted to deposits greater than 1 billion yen and a maturity of more than three months but less than two years) were introduced, and they were exempt from the TIRAL.

Maturity and denomination requirements of the above three instruments were gradually loosened during the late 1980s. In June 1989, term deposits with market interest rates were introduced at the retail level with the minimum amount of 0.5 million yen. The minimum-amount requirement was gradually reduced and finally abolished. In

October 1993, depository institutions were allowed to introduce deposits with floating rates and a maturity of more than three years. In order to segregate ordinary banks from long-term credit banks, ordinary banks were not allowed to accept deposits with a maturity of more than one year. Ordinary banks were allowed to introduce deposits with a maturity of one and one-half years in 1971, a maturity of two years in 1973, and a maturity of three years in 1981. Finally, in September 1994, all remaining interest-rate controls on deposit rates were abrogated.

[o] *Shinkin* banks are cooperatives for small and medium-sized companies; their lending is limited to members.

were based primarily on collateral requirements rather than cash-flow analysis, caused them to loosen credit standards as real-estate prices climbed.[6] In fact, in order to accelerate credit-check procedures for loan approval, many banks transferred the responsibility for loan-risk evaluation from their credit-investigation bureaus to less independent monitoring bureaus reporting directly to the banks' sales divisions.

Collapse of the Bubble

Following consecutive increases in the Bank of Japan's discount rate (Figure 1a), the highly overvalued Japanese stock market peaked at the end of 1989 (Figure 1b) and then collapsed after the summer of 1990. Meanwhile, in April 1990, the Ministry of Finance sought to contain the continuing rise in land prices by introducing guidelines limiting total bank lending to the real-estate sector (although the government later lifted the cap after the fall in real-estate prices). This move contributed to the leveling off of Japanese banks' asset growth, with total bank assets declining from 508 trillion yen in 1989 to about 491 trillion yen in 1990.[7] In 1992, officially monitored land prices began to decline (Figure 1c).

The subsequent slowdown in economic growth, together with the drastic decline in stock and real-estate prices, significantly weakened the banks and other financial institutions. This weakening manifested itself as follows: first, a 50 percent decline in the prices of property holdings by real-estate companies caused a rapid deterioration in the quality of loans to the real-estate industry; second, the value of collateral

[6] Cargill, Hutchison, and Ito (1997) have suggested that financial deregulation might have contributed to the speculative bubble of the 1980s.

[7] Here and throughout, "trillion" equals one million million; "billion" equals one thousand million.

TABLE 2

BANK LENDING BY SECTOR

(*Percent of total outstanding loans*)

	Individuals	Real Estate	Manufacturing	Construction	SMEs
1985	9.25	7.71	26.12	5.69	53.50
1986	9.79	9.61	23.58	5.52	56.57
1987	11.29	10.22	20.46	5.23	60.47
1988	12.86	11.14	19.09	5.26	64.46
1989	15.25	11.54	16.65	5.40	69.55
1990	16.27	11.28	15.74	5.31	70.36
1991	16.84	11.60	15.57	5.59	70.84
1992	16.78	12.08	15.06	5.94	71.12
1993	16.09	11.40	16.04	6.24	68.99
1994	15.94	11.69	15.64	6.41	69.48
1995	16.70	11.84	14.98	6.42	70.09
1996	17.32	12.19	14.56	6.32	70.31
1997	17.76	12.49	14.11	6.33	69.89
1998	18.42	12.77	14.33	6.47	69.20

SOURCE: Bank of Japan.
NOTE: The numbers do not include euro-yen loans.

eroded;[8] third, the decline in the value of the banks' equity holdings began to put pressure on bank capital; finally, the deceleration of economic growth reduced the ability of debtors to continue to service their loans.

The downgrading of Japanese banks by credit-rating agencies, which had begun in 1989, continued (Table 1). By 1992, many banks, which had previously enjoyed higher credit ratings than those of their corporate borrowers, saw their marginal costs of funding rising above the costs of many borrowers. This development, together with the incremental lifting of restrictions on the access of Japanese corporations to the domestic and euro bond markets, led to an acceleration in new bond issues (Figure 1d), exerting further pressure on the banks. Between 1984 and 1991, the percentage of funds raised by the corporate business sector through bond issues rose from 3.6 percent to 24.5 percent (Genay, 1993).

[8] For example, because prior to 1991, many borrowers could borrow up to 90 percent of the value of their real-estate collateral, the roughly 50 percent drop in real-estate prices between 1991 and 1998 meant that over 40 percent of such loans became uncovered.

FIGURE 1(a & b)

COLLAPSE OF THE BUBBLE

1a. Bank of Japan Discount Rate
(*Percent*)

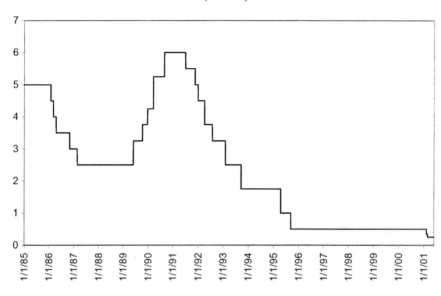

1b. Nikkei 225

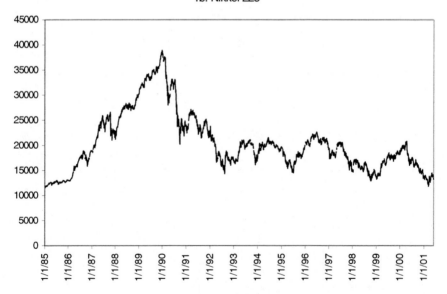

FIGURE 1(c & d)

COLLAPSE OF THE BUBBLE

1c. Nationwide, Urban Residential Land-Price Index

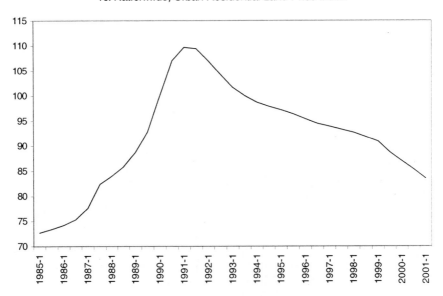

1d. Outstanding Corporate Straight Bonds
(*Billions of yen*)

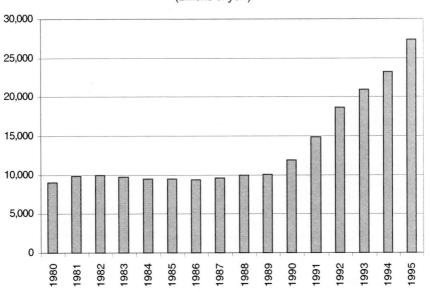

3 Existing Banking Regulations

The Basle Capital Accord

The Basle Capital Accord was fully implemented in March 1993 (the end of fiscal year 1992 in Japan). Although Japanese authorities required only those banks with international operations to comply with the 8 percent capital-adequacy requirement, many regional banks with no international operations also elected to adhere to it, rather than to the domestic 4 percent requirement.[9] Despite the sharp decline in Japanese stock prices, none of the banks experienced problems meeting the new capital requirement in March 1993. This was partly because the book value of the stocks they held were well below market valuation.[10] Although banks in Japan are prevented from owning more than 5 percent of the outstanding shares of any one company (Antimonopoly Law, Article 11), there is no ceiling on the total volume of stocks they may own. The market value of shares held by banks in March 1993 was 56.4 trillion yen, compared with the book value of only 34.5 trillion yen (Fukao, 1998). Even though regulations permitted banks to apply only 45 percent of these unrealized gains (amounting to 22 trillion yen) toward their Tier 2 capital,[11] these gains nevertheless accounted for about 25 percent of total bank capital in that year.

Loan Classification and Loan-Loss Provisioning

Since 1964, banks have been allowed to set up tax-deductible, general-reserve accounts for possible future loan losses. These reserve accounts, which differed from specific loan-loss reserves,[12] were intended to

---

[9] The calculation of the domestic capital-ratio requirement is different from the calculation under the international standard. For example, the calculation of the domestic requirement is not based on risk-weighted assets and does not allow the inclusion of noncore capital.

[10] The Japanese commercial code allows corporations to value stock holdings in their investment accounts at cost or at the lower of either cost or market value. Banks used the latter method before 1997.

[11] The distinction between Tier 1 and Tier 2 capital was used by the Basle Capital Accord to define the calculation of the capital requirement. Tier 1 capital is defined as common shares and retained earnings, whereas banks are allowed to include in their Tier 2 capital subordinated debt, general provision, and the unrealized reserves of some allowable assets (discussed below). Under the accord, both Tier 1 and Tier 2 capital can be used by banks to fulfill the 8 percent requirement, but the amount of Tier 2 capital used cannot exceed total Tier 1 capital.

[12] The purpose of the general-reserve account is for banks to provision against credit deterioration in the normal and substandard loan categories (the first and second

cover loans classified as "normal" and "substandard," and banks were not required to make any additional specific provisions against substandard loans. Banks had the option of either setting their general reserves to reflect their average loan loss during the previous three years or setting them at a reference level determined by the tax authorities and recommended by the regulatory authorities. Historically, banks often chose to set their general reserves at the reference level (fixed, after 1989, at 0.3 percent of total outstanding loans),[13] partly because, for most banks, the reference level was above their actual loan-loss experience. What is surprising is that the increase in nonperforming loans beyond 0.3 percent of total loans that occurred sometime during the 1990s did not cause banks voluntarily to increase their general reserves to take advantage of the available tax relief. This would suggest that either the banks did not want to transfer their Tier 1 capital to their Tier 2 accounts (especially when their Tier 2 capital was reaching the level of their Tier 1 capital) or that they felt that by raising their reserve accounts, they would be signaling the market that they expected further increases in nonperforming loans.[14] There may also have been a coordination problem among banks, with individual banks not wanting to draw attention to themselves by unilaterally raising their reserve accounts. If this was indeed the case, it raises questions as to why the authorities did not readjust the 0.3 percent reference level.[15]

For doubtful and loss loans, banks were expected to make specific provisions. Fifty percent of these specific provisions were tax deductible, but the guidelines for tax deductibility of specific provisioning were very stringent. In order to qualify loss loans for tax deductibility, for example, borrowers were required to maintain a negative net worth for a period of at least two years.

Banks were also very slow to write off loans that had a low probability of recovery. This was partly because the very strict tax guidelines

---

categories of the loan classification scheme). The specific-reserve account is intended to provision against loans in the "substandard," "doubtful," and "loss" categories.

[13] The ceiling for the reserve account was initially fixed at 0.42 percent of total loans in 1964 but was reduced five times, down to 0.3 percent by 1989, to reflect the downward trend of historical loan loss (Federation of Bankers Associations of Japan, 1989).

[14] Under the rules of the Basle Capital Accord (which Japanese authorities applied to Japanese banks), banks are allowed to count the general provision against loans toward Tier 2 capital up to the limit of 1.25 percent of risk-weighted assets.

[15] In 1997, the authorities eliminated the option of using the reference level from the tax regulations.

permitted write-offs only after the loan-loss amount had been ascertained in bankruptcy or foreclosure proceedings. In addition, some banks were reluctant to write off loans prior to bankruptcy proceedings, for fear that their borrowers might assume the banks had given up on loan recovery altogether and thus be prompted to stop repayment.

In January 1993, the Japanese banks established the Cooperative Credit Purchasing Company (CCPC). Although the CCPC was structured as an asset-management vehicle, the function of which is to purchase and undertake recovery of nonperforming loans, the apparent purpose behind its creation was to allow banks to take advantage of tax deductibility for bad loans. The tax authorities permitted banks to recognize the difference between the book value and preliminary price of loans sold to the CCPC as a tax-deductible expense.[16] It is important to point out that the CCPC's purchase of nonperforming loans is financed by corresponding loans from the selling banks to the CCPC, a scheme that succeeds only in replacing the residue value of a bad loan with another non-interest-bearing loan to the CCPC (Taniuchi, 1997). In short, although the CCPC gives the banks some tax relief for their nonperforming assets, it does little, if anything, to facilitate the asset-recovery process.[17]

4 Bank Strategy

Credit-Approval Procedures and Guidelines for New Loans

To adjust to the post-bubble economic environment, some banks returned the responsibility for loan-risk evaluation to their credit-investigation bureaus. Credit-approval procedures thus became more stringent, and more emphasis was placed on the borrower's cash-flow analysis, rather than on simple collateral requirements. Collateral value was more closely scrutinized, and the average loan-to-collateral ratio was, for many banks, considerably reduced. These changes suggest that, at least in the immediate aftermath of the bursting of the bubble, credit standards and conditions were significantly tightened. The Bank of Japan's Tankan survey shows that the willingness of financial institu-

---

[16] These transactions are made at an initial price (which is supposed to reflect fair market value), with the explicit agreement that their final price will be established after the CCPC has managed to sell the loans.

[17] By 1997, the CCPC had sold less than 5 percent of its portfolio.

tions to lend (as reported by enterprises) fell dramatically between 1990 and 1992 (Figure 2). At about the same time, growth in bank lending fell below growth in GDP (Table 3).

Forbearance and the Restructuring of Bad Loans

One of the cornerstones of the Japanese financial culture is the main-bank system. The main bank, delegated by other lenders, acts as a quasi-insider monitor of the borrowing firm and as a mediator when borrowers fall into stress (Aoki and Patrick, 1994; Fukuda and Hirota, 1996). The principal advantage of the main-bank system is the reduction of monitoring costs in the face of asymmetric information.[18] Until the 1990s, the main-bank system functioned reasonably well, with the main banks being responsible both for identifying problem borrowers before they became insolvent and for helping them restructure their businesses. Ex-employees of the main banks were often appointed as company directors by the borrowers so as to facilitate information exchange between the firms and the banks (Genay, 1993).

When the main banks themselves came under stress, however, the main-bank system became less effective. The banks were generally reluctant to allow their borrowers to default, not only because defaults

FIGURE 2

FINANCIAL INSTITUTIONS' WILLINGNESS TO LEND (TANKAN SURVEY)

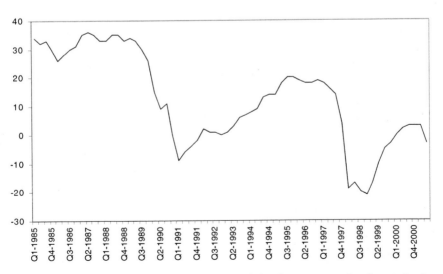

[18] Kawai, Hashimoto, and Izumida (1996) found that firms associated with main banks pay significantly lower interest-rate premia than firms not associated with main banks.

13

TABLE 3

CREDIT GROWTH OF DIFFERENT SECTORS
OF THE FINANCIAL SYSTEM
(Percent)

	GDP Growth	Banks	Other Banking Institutions[a]	Nonbank Financial Institutions[b]
1985	6.61	10.83	5.77	7.99
1986	4.69	9.49	8.75	7.37
1987	4.26	11.17	23.66	22.93
1988	6.92	10.94	15.15	22.85
1989	6.96	11.63	10.68	22.54
1990	7.51	9.21	9.91	21.10
1991	6.57	5.29	6.45	12.24
1992	2.79	2.33	9.09	5.55
1993	0.92	−1.12	6.41	5.44
1994	0.82	0.20	5.48	3.17
1995	0.83	1.68	0.98	−1.92
1996	3.44	1.17	3.69	7.03
1997	1.42	0.51	−2.29	−9.82
1998	−1.92	0.79	—	—

SOURCE: IMF, International Financial Statistics.

[a] "Other banking institutions" include specialized credit institutions, which cover resident foreign banks; financial institutions for small business; financial institutions for agriculture, forestry, and fishery; securities finance institutions and other private financial institutions; government financial institutions; the Trust Fund Bureau; postal savings; and postal annuity.

[b] Nonbank financial institutions comprise life- and non-life-insurance companies; the National Mutual Insurance Federation of Agricultural Cooperatives; and mutual insurance federations of agricultural cooperatives.

would reflect badly on their monitoring reputation in the loan market, but because a borrower's main bank is often required to absorb some of the losses incurred by other creditors. The banks therefore began to exercise forbearance, even when the long-term viability of their borrowers came into question. By the 1990s, Japanese banks were reportedly restructuring nonviable loans by reducing interest rates and extending their maturity. Banks also often capitalized unpaid interest and opened new credit lines so that borrowers could repay overdue loans. This was possible partly because the weakness of the loan-classification and provisioning requirements for restructured loans (and their enforcement) enabled banks to reclassify nonperforming loans as "performing" immediately after they were restructured.[19]

Banks also used "related companies" to clean up their balance sheets, taking advantage of a regulatory loophole that was closed only in December 1998.[20] Before that date, banks were required to consolidate and disclose, in their financial reporting, only those subsidiaries and affiliates in which they had a more than 50 percent or 20 percent stake, respectively. To circumvent the consolidation requirement, banks set up "related companies" that were neither subsidiaries nor affiliates, and to which they transferred their nonperforming loans at above-market value. These "related companies" were jointly owned by the banks (at shares of less than 5 percent) and the firms with which the banks had interlocking shares.

Increasing the Capital Base

Banks have two sources of capital: paid-in capital and retained earnings. During the 1980s, when bank-stock prices were high, many banks raised capital through public offerings in order to expand their lending in pace with the boom in the real-estate sector and to prepare for the implementation of the Basle Capital Accord. After the bubble burst, banks still tried to raise capital in the market, prompted by the need to increase their write-offs and to provision for rising nonperforming loans. Between 1992 and 1997, however, only Sakura Bank (1992 and 1994), Daiwa Bank (1994), Tokai Bank (1996), and Mitsubishi Bank (1995) were able to raise Tier 1 capital in the market. All these banks raised capital by issuing debt instruments that would convert into

---

[19] In the United States, for instance, banks are allowed to reclassify restructured loans as "performing" only after the borrowers have made three consecutive payments. Until then, interest payment is recognized only on a cash basis.

[20] Before December 1998, regulations for the purpose of consolidation and disclosure were specified as follows: the subsidiaries of banks (defined as companies in which banks have a more than 50 percent stake) must be consolidated in the financial reporting of banks on a line-by-line basis; the affiliates of banks (defined as companies in which banks have a more than 20 percent stake and also decisionmaking control) must be consolidated in the financial reporting of banks, using the equity method. In December 1998, these regulations were tightened to include (1) line-by-line consolidation: (a) between 40 and 50 percent of equity holding by a bank and "control" over the entity by the bank's "group," and (b) More than 50 percent equity holding by the bank's group and control over the entity by the group; (2) equity-method consolidation: (a) between 15 and 20 percent of equity holding by a bank and control by the bank's group, and (b) 20 percent or more equity holding by the bank's group and control by the group.

equity after several years.[21] These new, delayed-conversion, equity issues were apparently designed to "placate Japanese regulators who appeared to believe that ordinary equity issues would at least depress a bank's stock price, if not the level of Japanese stock prices in general" (Ammer and Gibson, 1996).[22] Ammer and Gibson and Ammer, Gibson, and Levy (1996) show that these banks had to pay a substantial premium to raise capital in this way; the Tokai Bank security issues, for example, were underpriced by at least 13 percent. By 1997, following the sharp decline in bank stocks (Figure 3) and consecutive downgrades by rating agencies of even the best banks, the banks suspended any further attempts to raise capital in the market.

Almost all of the banks issued subordinated debt, partly to compensate for the decline in Tier 2 capital caused by the drop in unrealized profits from securities holdings. When the credit ratings of Japanese banks fell, some banks offered these securities in private placements to institutional investors (such as insurance companies seeking relatively higher returns in a low-interest environment), as well as to nonaffiliate companies in their financial groups.[23] By 1997, however, the risk in subordination became apparent, and even subordinated debt issues fell out of favor with investors.

Arresting Eroding Margins

To compete with the commercial-paper and corporate-bond markets to which blue-chip Japanese corporations increasingly turned for their financing needs, the banks expanded their offerings of euro-yen loans to a wider base of borrowers; these loans, carrying lower interest rates than the domestic prime rate, had previously been extended only to blue-chip corporations with access to the international capital market. Concurrently, banks also started to expand their prime-rate offerings to

---

[21] Sakura Bank raised 200 billion yen through two convertible preferred stock issues (in March 1992 and April 1994), which were converted to common stock at maturity in June 1995 and October 1997. Daiwa Bank issued 50 billion yen of exchangeable bonds in March 1994, which were exchanged for common stock in March 1998. It also raised an additional 50 billion yen through a domestic private placement of convertible preferred stock with a thirty-year maturity. Tokai Bank raised 100 billion yen in 1996 through a euro-market issue of eight and one-half year convertible preference shares.

[22] The decline in Sakura's stock price around the time of its first of two equity issues may have "rattled" the regulators. In addition, banks have substantial exposure to each other's stock prices through their cross-shareholding arrangements (see Section 5).

[23] In Japan, banks are not allowed to use any subordinated debt issued by them to their affiliates toward their Tier 2 capital.

FIGURE 3

STOCK PRICES OF MAJOR BANKS

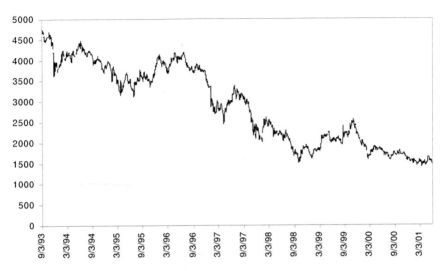

SOURCES: Bank of Japan and Reuters.

small and medium-sized enterprises that in the past could not have qualified for these loans. Although these initiatives may have slowed the decline in demand for bank credit, they eroded the short-term lending margins (Table 4), despite the fact that the continued decline in interest rates should have benefited banks' lending spreads.[24]

To protect their margins, banks began to take on more risk by, for example, extending the average maturity of their lending (Table 5). Between 1990 and 1997, loans with maturities of more than one year rose from about 56 percent to nearly 60 percent of total loans, whereas loans with maturities of less than three months declined from about 12 percent to 8 percent. These developments can be attributed to two factors. The first is that bank lending shifted from short-term working-capital finance to longer-term project finance—evidenced by the shift from loans on bills to loans on deeds (Table 6). This lengthening of loan maturity, which exposed banks both to more interest-rate risk and to

[24] Many banks, especially city banks, had a significant maturity mismatch between their assets and liabilities. This is partly because city (and regional) banks are not allowed to issue debentures and were not, until October 1993, allowed to offer deposits with maturities of more than three years. The result was that their overall interest margins expanded during declines in interest rates (Bank of Japan, 1996).

TABLE 4
INTEREST-RATE SPREADS
(Average percent)

	Time-Deposit Rates, 3–6 mos.[a]	New Lending Rates, Short-term[b]	Lending Spreads Short-Term	Time-Deposit Rates, 2–3 yrs.[a]	New Lending Rates, Long-Term[b]	Lending Spreads, Long-Term
1991	5.70	7.73	2.06	6.11	7.59	1.48
1992	3.10	5.65	2.48	4.59	5.89	1.30
1993	1.92	4.35	2.32	2.71	4.66	1.94
1994	1.61	3.53	1.80	2.02	3.91	1.89
1995	0.85	2.70	1.70	1.24	3.08	1.84
1996	0.22	2.03	1.63	0.65	2.50	1.85
1997	0.21	1.91	1.56	0.38	2.27	1.89
1998	0.19	1.88	1.55	0.30	2.21	1.91

SOURCE: Bank of Japan.

[a] There are deposits of less than 3 million yen. The rates exclude regulated interest rates.

[b] Short-term loans are loans with maturity of less than one year. Long-term loans are loans with maturity of more than one year.

TABLE 5
MATURITY STRUCTURE OF LOANS
(Percent of total loans)

	Less than 3 months	3 months to 1 year	More than 1 year	Others[a]
1985	21.2	33.8	39.0	6.0
1986	18.7	32.6	41.6	7.1
1987	17.7	28.9	44.7	8.7
1988	16.8	25.5	48.0	9.7
1989	12.6	23.9	52.7	10.8
1990	11.7	19.3	56.4	12.6
1991	11.2	19.0	56.4	13.4
1992	10.7	20.6	55.3	13.4
1993	9.7	21.1	55.9	13.3
1994	9.3	21.5	55.6	13.6
1995	8.8	19.8	58.2	13.2
1996	8.0	19.3	59.0	13.7
1997	8.2	18.6	59.2	14.0

SOURCE: Bank of Japan.

[a] "Others" are mainly overdraft loans.

TABLE 6

BILLS DISCOUNTED AND LOANS BY TYPE

(*Percent of total loans*)

	Bills Discounted[a]	Loans on Bills[b]	Loans on Deeds[c]	Over-drafts[d]
1989	6.83	27.56	52.11	13.50
1990	5.89	24.86	54.48	14.77
1991	5.63	23.62	54.52	16.23
1992	4.92	24.07	54.31	16.70
1993	4.75	23.96	54.51	16.78
1994	4.43	23.70	54.43	17.44
1995	4.03	22.48	55.94	17.54
1996	3.80	20.43	57.62	18.15
1997	3.52	19.52	57.90	19.06
1998	2.83	18.43	59.72	19.02

SOURCE: Bank of Japan.

[a] Bills discounted usually involves commercial bills issued by a third party. Company A receives from company B a promissory note, which company A discounts at a bank. These bills are generally short-term, with maturity of less than one year.

[b] Loans on bills are backed by bills issued by the borrower. These loans are structured so as to be repaid as the bills mature. The average maturity is less than one year. Companies have historically used this type of loan to finance their working capital.

[c] Loans on deeds are loans with a written contract. They generally carry a maturity of between three to five years. Companies typically use these loans to finance medium- and long-term investments.

[d] Overdraft loans carry a commitment by banks to provide loans up to a prespecified ceiling. These loans are typically used by borrowers to finance short-term liquidity needs.

liquidity risk,[25] is probably the reason why average spreads on long-term lending did not fall, as spreads on short-term lending did (Table 4). The second factor (discussed above) is that problem loans were restructured.[26]

[25] Under the loans on bills arrangement, banks can always sell their holdings of bills in the secondary market (including to the Bank of Japan in its repurchase operations). Securitization of loans on deeds, although possible, has not become as common as it is in the United States.

[26] It is difficult to evaluate the relative importance of these two factors. It can be argued, however, that the fact that capital investment was stagnant for most of the 1990s undercuts the importance of the shift in lending.

To boost short-term profits, the banks also relaxed credit conditions, as shown by the steady increase until the mid-1990s in unsecured loans, a reversal of the previous trend (Table 7). Another indication of relaxed credit conditions is the continued migration of loans during this period from loans on bills to loans on overdrafts, because the conditions for loans on bills are more stringent than those for overdraft loans.[27]

A recent paper by Woo (1999) suggests that, until 1995, weakly capitalized banks expanded their lending more rapidly than strongly

TABLE 7

BANK LOANS BY TYPE OF SECURITY
(Percent of total loans)

	Secured by Real Estate	Secured by Stocks and Bonds	Secured by Others[a]	Secured by Third-Party Guarantee	Unsecured
1985	21.72	1.96	9.57	26.31	40.44
1986	22.08	2.17	9.87	25.97	39.91
1987	23.19	2.35	9.43	25.61	39.41
1988	23.86	2.62	9.18	26.76	37.59
1989	25.69	2.63	8.31	29.31	34.06
1990	27.22	2.31	8.60	29.93	31.94
1991	28.08	1.91	8.29	30.32	31.41
1992	28.41	1.65	8.11	29.69	32.12
1993	27.93	1.66	8.16	29.93	32.32
1994	26.93	1.52	8.01	30.47	33.08
1995	25.36	1.53	7.90	31.83	33.37
1996	24.08	1.30	7.68	32.86	34.08
1997	23.46	1.38	7.46	34.07	33.63

SOURCE: Bank of Japan.
[a] "Others" includes deposits.

[27] Whereas clearinghouses for bills and checks block any further access to the clearing facility of issuers of bills who miss two consecutive payments, overdraft loans provide borrowers with more flexibility for repayment. And while the rollover of loans on bills must be requested and approved, the rollover of an overdraft is, in practice, automatic. The overdraft facility also gives lenders more discretion in classifying the loans. The rise in overdraft loans might thus be interpreted as an accumulation of disguised nonperforming loans. This seems especially so if we project the aggregate size of overdraft loans to the situation of individual borrowers. Overdraft loans are designed to provide liquidity and thus should fluctuate according to the borrowers' receipts and payments; if they are rising at the level of each individual borrower (for which numbers are not available) as they are at the aggregate level, it would suggest that banks have been accommodating the deterioration of their borrowers' liquidity conditions.

capitalized banks did. The paper's cross-sectional regressions show that bank lending was negatively correlated with bank capital in the early 1990s, despite the introduction of the Basle Capital Standard.[28] Woo argues that this phenomenon is reminiscent of the "gamble for resurrection" of the insolvent U.S. savings and loans in the 1980s and might be attributable to the relative laxity of the regulatory environment, particularly the lack of pressure on banks with declining capital to restrain their asset growth.

Tapping Unrealized Capital Gains

With shrinking margins and increasing numbers of nonperforming loans to provision and write off, banks had to tap into the unrealized gains on their holdings of bonds, stocks, and real estate. Many banks liquidated bond holdings the unrealized gains of which had been boosted by the declining market interest rates. Many also realized the hidden capital gains on their real-estate holdings by selling their office space outright and then leasing it back. In some cases, the gains were very substantial, because the banks had owned these properties for several decades. As a result of these real-estate sales, the book value of land and property held by Japanese banks shrank from more than 10 trillion yen to about 3 trillion yen between 1995 and 1998 (Table 8).[29]

Because 100 percent of realized capital gains could be applied to offset pretax losses,[30] as opposed to only 45 percent of unrealized gains counted toward Tier 2 capital, banks also tapped into the unrealized gains on their stock holdings. This strategy became especially attractive when increased provisioning and write-offs caused the banks' Tier 1 capital to decline relative to their Tier 2 capital (Figure 4).[31] There are, however, limitations to this method of boosting book capital. Japanese corporate borrowers and their main banks had, over the years, developed a culture of cross-shareholding as part of their long-term business relations. Banks were often compelled, therefore, to

[28] American banks, facing the new Bank for International Settlements (BIS) capital standard in this period, curtailed their lending.

[29] Because the book value and market value of the banks' real-estate holdings differed significantly, the actual realized gains from the liquidation of these holdings were far greater than the change in their book value.

[30] When banks realize 100 percent of hidden gains in stocks by selling them in the market, these capital gains, treated as income, are taxed at the effective tax rate of approximately 50 percent.

[31] As already mentioned, under the Basle Capital Accord, Tier 2 capital can be applied toward the capital requirement only up to the level of Tier 1 capital.

TABLE 8

BANK HOLDINGS OF REAL ESTATE AND UNREALIZED GAINS,
1995–1998
(*Billions of yen*)

	Bank Holdings of Land and Buildings	Unrealized Gains on Investment Securities	Unrealized Gains on Stocks
1991	5,573	110,703	81,622
1992	7,724	128,968	91,966
1993	8,078	177,671	125,467
1994	7,522	86,526	53,309
1995	10,651	132,976	101,550
1996	9,255	64,436	47,579
1997	8,944	12,420	10,609
1998	3,385	n.a.	n.a.

SOURCE: Bank Scope (Fitch IBCA).

NOTE: To exclude the effect of closed banks during this period, the sample includes only banks that operated continuously between 1995 and 1998.

repurchase, at market price, the stocks they sold. This meant both that the book value of the stocks was increased, reducing the return on assets (unrealized capital gains were not counted toward bank assets)

FIGURE 4

DISCREPANCY BETWEEN TIER 1 AND TIER 2 CAPITAL

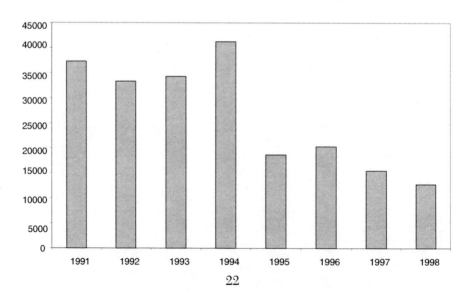

and that bank capital became more susceptible to stock-price fluctuation because of the requirement that stocks be accounted for at the lower of either cost or market valuation. In any case, by 1997, banks had largely exhausted the unrealized gains on their securities holdings (Table 8).[32]

5   Corporate Governance of Japanese Banks

To understand the rapidity with which the financial conditions of Japanese banks deteriorated, it is important to examine the issue of their corporate governance. It has recently been suggested that the failure of corporate governance is one of the key factors behind the Japanese banking crisis (Fukao, 1998).

Major Shareholders

The corporate governance system of Japanese banks is largely determined by the structure of bank ownership. Although bank shares are widely held, relatively few shareholders own the majority of the total outstanding shares. For example, the thirty largest shareholders of Bank of Tokyo-Mitsubishi accounted for more than 40 percent of its outstanding shares in March 1999. A typical Japanese bank has four groups of major shareholders:

• Japanese life-insurance companies, which are among the largest institutional investors in the world, reflecting, in part, the very high savings rate in Japan. The life-insurance companies own bank shares both for investment and for good business relations with the banks, the employees and customers of which buy insurance products. Life-insurance companies are also large holders of subordinated debt issued by banks.

• Corporate borrowers, with which Japanese banks have developed a system of cross-shareholding in order to reinforce their long-term business commitments. Although these cross-shareholding arrangements weakened steadily throughout the 1990s, as large corporations turned increasingly to the capital market for their funding, corporate

---

[32] The ratio of bank-stock holdings to their core capital was about 300 percent for long-term credit banks and about 200 percent for city banks. A study by Nikko Research Center, issued in January 1997, showed that a further decline in the Nikkei average to the 13,000 and 18,000 range could have wiped out the unrealized capital gains of the twenty major banks.

23

borrowers still account for about 50 percent of the total outstanding shares of Japanese banks.[33]

• Bank employees, who acquire shares in their banks through employee stock-participation plans. It is also usually expected that retired bank employees, nominated as board directors, will have some holdings in the banks. Bank employees are often among the largest shareholders of regional banks.

• Other banks. Japanese banks also developed a system of cross-shareholding—especially between city banks and regional banks—that was perhaps originally conceived as a way to expand their business base and to fend off hostile takeovers by foreign banks, once foreign investors had gained access to the Japanese capital markets.

Shareholders and Corporate Governance

The ownership structure described above has produced a largely ineffectual corporate-governance system in which shareholders have only modest control over the management of banks. The influence of mutual life insurers (the largest shareholders of most major banks),[34] for example, is limited by the insurers' own corporate-governance problems (Fukao, 1988).[35] As for the borrower-shareholders of the banks, the fact that bank credit has, for most of them, remained their principal source of funding weakens their position as shareholders.[36] This is especially true when these borrower-shareholders are themselves under stress and depend on the banks to finance their restructuring. Even the healthy borrower-shareholders are more interested in favorable terms for their borrowing than in high returns from their bank-stock holdings.

The lack of incentive for shareholders to exercise their corporate-governance power also applies to the employee-shareholders of the banks. The interdependency between corporate management and employees in the Japanese employment system often results in the

---

[33] This aspect of Japanese banking makes banks resemble listed credit cooperatives (Irvine, 1998).

[34] In Japan, most life-insurance companies are structured as mutual companies.

[35] This is related to the fact that policy holders are nominal owners of the mutual life insurers and may number in the tens of thousands.

[36] Nonfinancial companies in Japan financed about 62 percent of their liabilities and equity through borrowing in 1998, as opposed to 13 percent in the United States (Bank of Japan, 1999).

employees siding with management. In addition, the employee-shareholders tend to prefer wages to dividends because they are taxed twice on the latter. In theory, of course, there is no reason why banks as shareholders of other banks should not exercise their corporate-governance role, especially because they have additional exposure to each other through their interbank activities. However, many banks have found themselves in similar circumstances, and the "convoy system," a strategy designed by the authorities to use good banks to help bail out bad banks, has weakened their ability to exercise their shareholder rights. In short, this kind of ownership structure implies that bank management may often count on the support of most of its shareholders and has little trouble in proxy solicitations or at shareholders' meetings; it is very rare for "silent majorities" to vote against management's decisions.[37]

The composition of boards of directors also contributes to the weakness of bank corporate governance. Board members are typically "promoted" from the ranks of employees and generally do not see their roles as representing shareholders' interests. It is rare for Japanese banks to appoint external directors from other than those companies with which they have long-term business relationships. Moreover, board members are expected to resign when their terms expire, so that junior employees can replace them. This system gives little incentive for board members to take decisive action regarding problems their banks may face, so long as nothing goes wrong during their tenure.

Internal and External Auditors

Japanese corporate law provides for both external and internal auditors. In reality, however, their roles are very limited. Internal auditors are appointed from among former bank employees, a fact that may significantly limit their independence. External auditors are generally reluctant to express opinions about their corporate clients' financial statements for fear of losing them. This situation has been exacerbated in Japan, because accountants have rarely been deemed liable for approving financial statements that misrepresented a company's business conditions. Recently, however, shareholders and creditors of failed financial institutions have begun to sue such accountants for compensation.

---

[37] The number of individual investors is generally small. For example, individual shareholders account for less than 10 percent of Bank of Tokyo-Mitsubishi's outstanding shares.

Consequences

Weak corporate governance has had two profound and detrimental effects on the Japanese banking system:

• Bank management is not under pressure to maximize profitability. Instead, management focuses on market share and on providing stable employment and services for clients.[38] The average yields on working assets of Japanese banks, together with their returns on assets and their returns on equity, were among the lowest in the industrialized world during the 1990s (Figure 5). Weak profitability means that when loans go bad, banks lack sufficient retained earnings to absorb them and, furthermore, that they have problems raising new capital in the market when their capital declines *pari passu* with write-offs and provisioning.

• The absence of checks and balances (accountability) means that bank management has no incentive to restructure and that it will likely postpone dealing with problems during its tenure. This is one of the reasons why bank management has failed to take a proactive stance with regard to the increasing volume of nonperforming loans, a reticence that has unnecessarily prolonged the crisis. Weak internal and external audits, moreover, have made it possible for bank managers to conceal their problems.[39]

6   The Beginning of the Crisis

It was partly because of weak corporate governance that most banks failed to take appropriate measures to adjust to the new economic conditions of the 1990s, preferring, instead, to wait for stock and property prices to return to their precollapse levels (Taniuchi, 1997). Although most of the financial system managed to hang on until at least 1995, the problems facing the *jusen* companies (the housing-loan corporations) were already publicly recognized by early 1992.

---

[38] The chairman of one Japanese bank was quoted as saying: "Our purpose is to serve clients and Japanese industry. There must be profit, but profit must be reasonable. If we make too much profit, we are eating the profits of our clients" (Irvine, 1998).

[39] Former executives of the now defunct Long Term Credit Bank of Japan and Nippon Credit Bank are currently facing trials for fraudulent accounting and false disclosure related to the recognition of losses for nonperforming loans at their banks.

FIGURE 5
RETURNS AND YIELDS ON EQUITY AND ASSETS

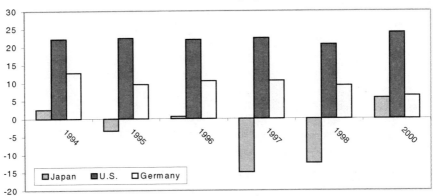

Returns on Equity

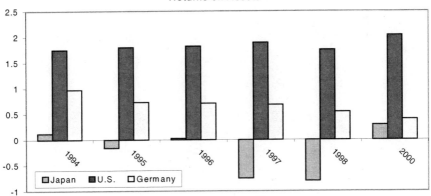

Returns on Assets

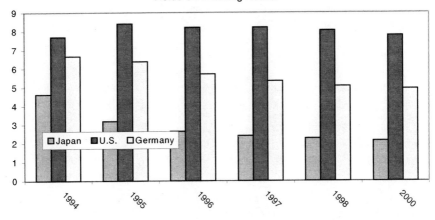

Yields on Working Assets

The Jusen Companies

The *jusen* companies were established in the mid-1970s by banks, securities companies, and insurance companies to engage in home-mortgage lending. Displaced by banks from the home-mortgage market in the 1980s, they found their way to real-estate lending in the second half of the decade and, by the beginning of the 1990s, had made the real-estate sector their primary market. Funded by agricultural cooperatives, which were exempt from the Ministry of Finance's April 1990 restrictions on real-estate lending, *jusen* lending to the real-estate sector grew sharply in 1990–91.

Concerns about the quality of *jusen* lending grew during 1992, and in the spring of 1993, creditors and owners of *jusen* companies agreed to implement a ten-year rehabilitation plan with the support of the Ministry of Finance. The plan, which consisted of reduced interest rates on outstanding loans to the *jusen* companies and additional liquidity injection by the creditors, was predicated on the assumption of a recovery of the real-estate market over a ten-year period. Instead, real-estate prices fell even further. In August 1995, after the Ministry of Finance conducted a special examination of the *jusen* companies,[40] the ministry, the creditors, and the owners of seven *jusen* companies agreed to dissolve the firms. In the spring of 1996, the Diet passed a plan to inject government funds to facilitate their liquidation, and in July, the Housing Loan Administration Corporation was established to assume their assets and liabilities. The shortfall in assets was borne mainly by the parent banks and creditor banks of the *jusen* companies. The parent banks wrote off all their equity stakes and loans to the companies (worth 3.5 trillion yen), and other creditor banks wrote off about 1.7 trillion yen in loans.[41]

Early Bankruptcies

Toward the end of 1994, the Tokyo metropolitan government suspended the operations of two insolvent credit cooperatives, the Tokyo Kyowa Credit Cooperative and the Anzen Credit Cooperative. Subse-

---

[40] The examination revealed that 74 percent of the *jusen* loans were nonperforming.

[41] The agricultural cooperatives, however, which as a group had the largest exposure to the *jusen* companies, were fully reimbursed in the settlement, partly because of their political clout. The Ministry of Agriculture maintained that forcing agricultural cooperatives to incur losses would have had serious consequences for these institutions, which not only are credit institutions but also provide joint purchasing, marketing, and distribution services to farmers.

quently, Tokyo Kyodo Bank was established (with capital participation of the Bank of Japan, commercial banks, and credit cooperatives) to liquidate the cooperatives. The resolution of these two cooperatives marked a clear departure from the authorities' previous policy of not allowing any depository institution to fail. Indeed, by 1995, the authorities, which had previously encouraged existing financial institutions ("white knights") to acquire those in serious distress, could no longer find any institution that was willing or strong enough to fulfill such a role.

In July 1995, the Tokyo metropolitan government ordered Cosmo Credit Cooperative to suspend new deposit-taking and lending operations. In August 1995, the Osaka prefectural government issued the same order to Kizu Credit Cooperative. These cooperatives had expanded their business so rapidly during the 1980s (primarily by lending to the real-estate industry), that by the time of their closure, they had become de facto full-range banks.

"Regulatory arbitrage" was one of the main factors behind the failure of the credit cooperatives. These cooperatives, supervised by the prefectural governments, were subject to looser supervision and regulation than was applied to banks, a fact that allowed them to engage in riskier banking activities than the latter. With the relaxation of restrictions on their lending to nonmembers, the cooperatives contributed to an unhealthy competition in the credit market, which in turn indirectly weakened all the financial institutions.[42]

In August 1995, the Ministry of Finance ordered Hyogo Bank, a regional bank, to suspend new deposit taking and lending; subsequently, its business was transferred to the newly established Midori Bank. By this time, it was clear that the supervisory authorities had no choice but to close insolvent financial institutions. Depositors (institutional depositors in particular) reacted by transferring their deposits from banks with low credit ratings to those with higher credit ratings or to the postal savings system (Table 9). The ensuing segmentation of the deposit market and the interbank market required depository institutions with low credit ratings to offer higher interest rates to attract funding.

The failures of these institutions provided the impetus to create a framework to use public money to resolve failed institutions and to

---

[42] This was also the case with the agricultural and fishery cooperatives, which were supervised by the Ministry of Agriculture, Forestry, and Fishery.

TABLE 9

DEPOSITS GROWTH AT DIFFERENT
FINANCIAL INSTITUTIONS
(*Percent*)

	City Banks	Credit Coop- eratives	Postal Savings
1991	–4.84	0.23	14.18
1992	–6.05	2.65	9.31
1993	1.29	3.33	7.90
1994	1.95	4.11	7.66
1995	3.03	–5.40	8.02
1996	0.06	–3.23	5.36
1997	2.86	–3.34	6.96

SOURCE: Bank of Japan.
NOTE: Deposits are from the private sector and include deposits by other financial institutions.

extend protection to all depositors in all credit cooperatives.[43] In June 1996, the Diet passed six laws, establishing the Housing Loan Administration Corporation and the Resolution Collection Bank (which took over the Tokyo Kyodo Bank), which were designed to cope with the liquidation and the recovery of assets of failed *jusen* companies and credit cooperatives. The new laws also strengthened the deposit-insurance scheme.[44]

Regulatory Weakness and Forbearance

That the flow of deposits from weak banks to stronger banks did not become even more pronounced was largely attributable to the belief of most Japanese depositors that the government would fully guarantee

[43] Political and popular opposition was deemed to be too great, however, to expand the scheme to cover ordinary banks. Deposit-insurance funds could contribute to the resolution of a bank only to the extent that would have been required under a payoff scenario. Indeed, because of this limitation, Midori Bank had to assume nonperforming loans of the defunct Hyogo Bank that could not be written off by contribution from the deposit-insurance fund.

[44] The Deposit Insurance Corporation established the Financial Stabilization Fund (with funds provided by private financial institutions) and made a capital subscription of 200 billion yen to the Housing Loan Administration Corporation (using 100 billion yen each from the Financial Stabilization Fund and the Bank of Japan).

their deposits. By choosing not to openly dispel this notion, the government would eventually have no choice but to fulfill the public's expectations.

As the implicitly assumed guarantor of bank liabilities, the government should have had an interest in minimizing the potential fiscal cost of bank restructuring. It can be argued, however, that the government's strategy until 1997, that is, to postpone restructuring, actually raised the fiscal cost of the banks' final resolution.

Between 1990 and 1995, the authorities did little to arrest the decline in the conditions of the banking system. This reflected, to a great extent, a false hope that the economy would soon turn the corner and that a full economic recovery would buoy up the banks (Nishimura, 1999). After 1995, it was quite clear that the banks' problems had considerably worsened and that a more systematic public intervention would eventually become inevitable. Regulators still hesitated to take strong action, however, for fear of triggering a public panic, especially in the absence of an adequate deposit-insurance scheme and a legal framework for bank restructuring that could deal with a full-blown banking crisis. Until 1997, therefore, the regulators are thought to have exercised forbearance.[45] Although there is no explicit evidence supporting the theory of regulatory forbearance, a number of observations suggest that the hypothesis cannot be easily rejected:

• The regulatory authorities, who had the power to delicense banks, intervened only after the distressed banks had become insolvent, a delay implying that they acted only when they had no other alternative. The Tokyo metropolitan government, for example, already knew, after a special examination in the spring of 1993, that the Tokyo Kyowa Credit Cooperative and Anzen Credit Cooperative were insolvent, but it did not close them until the end of 1994. Cargill, Hutchison, and Ito (1997) point out that both deposits and lending of the Tokyo Kyowa Credit Cooperative and Anzen Credit Cooperative nearly doubled between March 1992 and November 1994. The majority of the new loans made during this period eventually became nonperforming.

---

[45] Many senior bureaucrats from the Ministry of Finance and the Bank of Japan move, on retirement, into high positions at commercial banks. Known as *amakudari* (in literal translation, "descent from heaven"), these appointments are intended sometimes as rewards for retiring officials and sometimes as part of the authorities' attempt to arrest the worsening of distressed banks. Critics have pointed out that this system, by creating an interdependent relationship between the supervisors and the supervised, inevitably leads to conflicts of interest and constrains the actions of the supervisors (Hsu, 1994).

• Banks were allowed to continue to pay dividends even after it was evident that retained earnings were needed to strengthen their capital base and to help provision for loan losses. Because the tradition of paying low but consistent dividends regardless of company performance has been a widespread corporate practice in Japan, the banks and regulatory authorities believed that suspending dividend payments would be a sign of distress that would lead to a sharp fall in the prices of bank stocks or possibly even to runs on the banks. Thus, banks continued to pay dividends for several years, even when they recorded negative net profits. Table 10 shows that, in 1991, Japanese banks together paid out 750 billion yen in dividends from a combined net profit of 2.3 trillion yen. By 1997, after the banks had lost about 9 trillion yen, they still paid out dividends of 680 billion yen.

• In Japan, guidelines issued by the Tokyo Stock Exchange require that listed corporations be delisted if they incur negative income for three consecutive years. In 1995, banks incurred a combined loss of 5 trillion yen, after setting aside 23 trillion yen for provisioning. In 1996, banks tried to avoid reporting losses, so as not to be delisted in 1997 if they suffered additional setbacks . The banks therefore reduced their provisioning by half in 1996 in order to report a small profit (Table 10) and raised provisioning again only in 1997. The fact that nonperforming loans continued to rise throughout the late 1990s suggests that the provisioning requirement was not rigorously enforced.

• Loan-classification rules were lax compared to international standards of best practice, and banks and regulators consequently took too long to recognize the extent of nonperforming loans in the system. When, at the end of March 1998, major banks used the more stringent U.S.-related standards for reporting, their nonperforming loans were about 50 percent greater than those reported under the old system (Levy, 1998).

7 Resolution Strategy

The Failure of Major Financial Institutions

Several high-profile financial institutions went into effective bankruptcy in 1997. In April, the Ministry of Finance ordered Nissan Life Insurance, one of the nationwide insurance companies, to suspend its operations. In November, Sanyo Securities, a second-tier securities firm, filed an application for rehabilitation. On the same day, Sanyo also defaulted on its borrowing in the call market, the first such occurrence

TABLE 10

AGGREGATED BANK-INCOME STATEMENT

(*Billions of yen*)

	1991	1992	1993	1994	1995	1996	1997	1998[a]
Net interest revenue	14,618	19,189	18,456	19,539	19,523	19,080	17,408	10,562
Other operating income	4,649	4,648	6,269	5,670	6,853	5,272	6,740	3,386
Overheads	13,193	15,332	15,593	16,654	14,474	14,744	14,888	10,526
Loan-loss provision	1,650	3,897	9,163	12,544	23,342	11,532	25,809	21,202
Others	982	6	3,163	5,610	6,534	2,160	6,243	7,790
Before-tax profits	5,410	4,616	3,131	1,619	−4,905	236	−10,304	−9,990
Tax	3,045	2,780	1,618	1,347	442	597	−619	−2,515
Net income	2,367	1,835	1,515	271	−5,346	−360	−9,683	−7,474
Dividend paid	750	864	875	892	710	675	687	343

SOURCE: Bank Scope.

[a] 1998 data are preliminary.

in Japanese history.[46] This default led to a sharp curtailment of inter-bank activities. In the same month, the Ministry of Finance ordered Hokkaido Takushoku Bank, one of the city banks, and Yamaichi Securities to suspend their operations. Both eventually closed. These developments led to a sell-off of bank shares in the Tokyo stock market and to an increase in the cost of funding of Japanese banks in the overseas interbank markets (the so called "Japan premium").

The Authorities' Response

In 1997, the Japanese authorities introduced, under the Law to Ensure the Soundness of Financial Institutions, the Prompt Corrective Action (PCA) framework, modeled loosely on the American framework (Table 11). The PCA, which was introduced on a preliminary basis in 1997 and was to take full effect in April 1998, has two main components. It introduces a self-assessment process that holds the banks themselves

[46] Securities firms are allowed to participate in the interbank market, although there is a limit on the amount they can borrow. Insurance companies are allowed to participate in the interbank market as providers of funds.

TABLE 11

SUMMARY OF PROMPT CORRECTIVE ACTION PROVISIONS: JAPAN AND THE UNITED STATES

| Japan | | United States | | |
Capital Ratios[a]	Regulatory Actions	Capital Ratios[b]	Mandatory Actions	Discretionary Actions
n. a.	n. a.	"Adequately capitalized": total ≥ 8 percent and Tier 1 ≥ 4 percent and leverage ratio < 4 percent	Disallow brokered deposits except with FDIC approval.	None
< 8 percent for banks with international operations; < 4 percent for banks without international operations	Order formulation and implementation of management improvement plans	"Undercapitalized": total < 8 percent or Tier 1 < 4 percent or leverage ratio < 4 percent	Suspend dividends and management fees. Require capital-restoration plan. Restrict asset growth. Require approval for acquisitions, branching, and new activities. Disallow brokered deposits.	Order recapitalization. Restrict interaffiliate transactions. Restrict deposit interest rates.
< 4 percent for banks with international operations; < 2 percent for banks without international operations	Order recapitalization plans. Impose restraints on asset growth. Impose ban on new activities and branches and limits on current activities. Impose ban on new subsidiaries and overseas affiliates and limits on the current activities of such entities. Limit dividend payments. Limit bonus payments to directors	"Significantly undercapitalized": total < 6 percent or Tier 1 < 3 percent or leverage ratio < 3 percent	Same as above. In addition, order recapitalization. Restrict interaffiliate transactions. Restrict deposit interest rates. Restrict pay of officers.	Same as above. In addition, order conservatorship or receivership if bank fails to submit or implement a plan to recapitalize. Improve any provision for "critically undercapitalized" banks if necessary.

	Japan	United States
	< 0 percent for banks with international operations; < 0 percent for banks without international operations	"Critically undercapitalized": tangible equity to total assets ratio of ≤ 2 percent	n.a.
	and management. Limit deposit interest rates. Suspend all or part of banking business. This order can be replaced with lesser action if (1) the net value of assets, including unrealized gains, is positive; (2) the net value including unrealized gains is negative but expected to be positive after considering (a) the implementation of management improvement plans and other specific measures; (b) business income and profitability; (c) the bad-asset ratio. A business suspension order can be issued at any time when the net value of the assets, including unrealized losses is, or is expected to be, negative.	Same as above. In addition, order receivership or conservatorship within 90 days. Order receivership if critically undercapitalized for four quarters. Suspend payments on subordinated debt. Restrict certain other activities.	

SOURCES: Japan: Ministry of Finance; United States: Federal Deposit Insurance Corporation.

a. The international capital standards (BIS capital-adequacy standards) apply to banks with international operations. The adjusted national capital standards apply to banks with purely domestic operations.

b. The total capital ratio cited is the total risk-weighted capital; the leverage ratio is the ratio of Tier 1 capital to total assets.

responsible for valuing their assets on a prudent and realistic basis, according to well-defined guidelines. These procedures require that the banks' own findings (including the necessary provisioning for loan losses and capital ratios) be subject to review by external auditors and to inspection and monitoring by bank examiners. The PCA also specifies the capital-ratio thresholds under which regulators can order banks to take remedial action, ranging from the reduction of branches and dividends to liquidation in the case of insolvency. These thresholds significantly narrow the scope for regulatory forbearance by putting pressure on the regulators to act when a bank weakens.

It also became clear in 1997 that, despite the authorities' assurances to the contrary, even very large financial institutions were not too big to fail. This realization and the perception of weakness in other banks in the system prompted depositors to withdraw their funds more aggressively from weakened depository institutions.[47] On November 26, 1997, the Minister of Finance, Mr. Hiroshi Mitsuzuka, declared that the government would guarantee, until the end of March 2001, the full amounts of (both yen and foreign-currency) deposits, debentures by banks, and certain kinds of trusts offered by trust banks, regardless of the limited coverage under the deposit-insurance system.

By 1998, the severity of the problems faced by the banking system, and the need to use public funds to restructure it, were finally recognized by the public and lawmakers alike. In February 1998, the Diet passed two laws to amend the Deposit Insurance Law and to establish emergency measures for stabilizing the financial system. The new laws authorized the provision of 30 trillion yen to bail out banks and protect depositors.[48] Although these measures were steps in the right direction, they were only incremental, and the banking supervisory authorities were still not sufficiently equipped to deal with the magnitude of the problem.

In March 1998, when many banks experienced difficulties in meeting the capital requirement, all the major banks applied for injections of public capital. Because weak banks did not want to draw attention to themselves by applying for more capital than the stronger banks requested, most of the banks applied for the same amount of 100 billion

---

[47] Although depositors had not played an active role in the corporate governance of banks until the late 1990s, their sharply increased withdrawals from weak financial institutions in 1997 forced the government to deal with the banking-sector problems.

[48] Seventeen trillion yen were earmarked for dealing with bank failures up until March 2001; the remaining 13 trillion were earmarked for recapitalization of banks through the purchase of preferred shares and subordinated debt.

yen. The Bank of Tokyo-Mitsubishi, which had reportedly been reluctant to apply for capital injection (so as to avoid any government intervention in the management of its business), was, as the head of the Tokyo Bankers' Association in 1997, the first to announce its application for capital injection. The government subsequently injected 1.8 trillion yen (0.4 percent of GDP) into these banks, mainly in the form of subordinated debt.

To help banks further strengthen their capital positions, if only on the books, the authorities relaxed accounting rules, allowing banks to count 45 percent of their revalued real-estate holdings toward their Tier 2 capital (Table 12). In addition, recognizing that the market value of the stock holdings of many banks had fallen below their cost, the authorities allowed banks to adopt cost-basis accounting in place of the lower of either cost or market accounting for equity securities held for investment purposes.[49]

Credit Crunch

The year 1997 marked a turning point for the Japanese banking system. Characterized by increased distress in the financial system and by heightened regulatory pressure and market scrutiny of the banking system, 1997 culminated in a fundamental shift in banks' lending behavior. Woo (1999) finds that the cross-sectional correlation between the growth in bank lending and bank capital, which had been negative for most of the early 1990s, became positive in 1997, a change suggesting that weak banks, constrained by their capital positions, began to grow less rapidly than better capitalized banks. Woo also finds that capital weakness tended to constrain growth in bank lending more than growth in bank assets, indicating that the slowdown in bank lending was not entirely due to their funding capacity.

Woo attributes this phenomenon in some measure to the increased failures of distressed financial institutions in 1997, failures that substantially abated the moral-hazard problem in the system by signaling a fundamental shift in the government's strategy for dealing with ailing institutions. Regardless of the motivations for this change in strategy (whether prompted by the government's realization that its resources for rescuing the banking system were limited or by its resolve to introduce some discipline into the system), it gave credibility to the

---

[49] The new regulations did not, however, allow banks that opted for the cost-basis accounting rule to count unrealized gains on stock securities toward their Tier 2 capital.

TABLE 12

CAPITAL RATIOS UNDER OLD AND NEW ACCOUNTING STANDARDS FOR
THE NINETEEN MAJOR BANKS, MARCH 1997 AND MARCH 1998
(Percent)

	Capital Ratio			Tier 1 Capital Ratio		
	1997	1998 (old)	1998 (new)	1997	1998 (old)	1998 (new)
City Banks						
Tokyo-Mitsubishi[a]	9.28	8.20	8.54	4.97	4.27	4.27
Dai-Ichi Kangyo	8.76	7.51	9.09	4.38	3.76	4.63
Sakura	8.93	7.62	9.13	4.46	3.81	4.56
Sumitomo	8.75	8.33	9.23	4.5	4.17	4.76
Fuji	9.23	7.29	9.41	4.8	3.65	4.79
Sanwa	9.11	8.31	9.61	4.55	4.15	4.80
Tokai	9.09	8.82	10.26	4.55	4.41	5.41
Asahi	8.71	7.44	9.39	4.44	3.72	4.69
Daiwa	9.02	n.a.	10.30	4.73	3.56	5.35
Long-Term Credit Banks[a]						
Industrial Bank of Japan	9.04	9.31	9.74	4.83	4.79	4.95
LTCB of Japan	9.22	n.a.	10.32	4.61	3.82	5.16
Nippon Credit Bank	2.99	n.a.	n.a.	1.5	n.a.	n.a.
Trust Banks						
Mitsubishi[a]	9.68	n.a.	10.35	5.15	5.99	5.99
Sumitomo	8.97	n.a	9.90	5.45	4.22	5.27
Mitsui	9.56	8.66	10.41	5.35	4.33	6.02
Yasuda	9.87	n.a.	13.56	5.73	3.97	7.14
Toyo	10.02	9.29	10.68	5.79	4.64	5.78
Chuo	9.11	n.a.	12.73	4.93	5.03	7.95
Nippon	11.24	n.a.	9.83	10.29	8.21	9.26

SOURCES: Fitch IBCA, based on published financial statements as of May 22, 1998.

NOTES: The calculation for the old standards adjusts for the revaluation of real-estate holdings (45 percent of which can be included in Tier 2 capital under the new standards) as well as the change from the lower of cost or market accounting of unrealized equity securities holdings to cost-basis accounting from the old standards to the new standards.

[a] These three banks did not adopt the new accounting methods for unrealized equity securities holdings.

supervisory and regulatory framework and warned banks that they would suffer the same fate as the closed banks if they did not quickly restore soundness. The introduction of the PCA, and the fact that the capital ratios of weakly capitalized banks had come close to the 8 percent threshold, led the banks to cut back on their lending.[50] These findings are supported by two observations. First, the Tankan survey (Figure 2) suggests that the willingness of financial institutions to lend dropped significantly in 1997. Second, although lending by foreign banks in Japan contracted even more sharply than lending by domestic banks during the first half of the 1990s, foreign-bank lending surged in 1996 and accelerated in 1997, just when lending by Japanese banks started to contract (Table 13).[51]

The government responded to the ensuing "credit crunch" by increasing funding for the credit-guarantee schemes. Designed to help small and medium-sized companies gain access to the credit market, these schemes had been in place since 1953. Banks exploited the credit-guarantee schemes because they were allowed to attach a zero-risk weight to government-guarantee loans for the purpose of calculating

TABLE 13

CREDIT GROWTH OF DOMESTIC AND FOREIGN BANKS IN JAPAN

(*Millions of yen and percent*)

	Credits by Domestic Banks	Credit Growth of Domestic Banks	Credits by Foreign Banks in Japan	Credit Growth of Foreign Banks in Japan
1990	4,243,430	—	—	—
1991	4,458,893	5.08	121,462	—
1992	4,603,939	3.25	106,827	−12.05
1993	4,726,330	2.66	97,340	−8.88
1994	4,748,158	0.46	76,640	−21.27
1995	4,776,618	0.60	76,064	−0.75
1996	4,827,009	1.05	87,185	14.62
1997	4,823,121	−0.08	101,275	16.16
1998	4,779,785	−0.90	107,444	6.09

SOURCE: Bank of Japan.
NOTE: Data are for end of fiscal year.

[50] For example, banks reduced their lending to blue-chip Japanese corporations with which they had maintained close business ties over the years (the lending was, in any case, not profitable). Banks arranged for their security subsidiaries to help these corporations issue corporate bonds. Banks also cut back on their loans to overseas corporations with high credit ratings, especially after the yen started depreciating against the dollar.

[51] The migration of loans to blue-chip firms from Japanese banks to foreign banks was most noticeable for euro-yen loans.

TABLE 14
ACTIVITIES OF THE CREDIT-GUARANTEE CORPORATIONS
(Billions of yen)

	Guarantee Applications (During the Period)		Payment under Guarantee (During the Period)		Guarantee Obligation Outstanding	
	Number of cases	Value	Number of cases	Value	Number of cases	Value
1990	1,145,280	11,874	15,567	79	2,490,615	18,595
1991	1,196,422	12,189	19,822	145	2,676,463	21,216
1992	1,365,306	13,747	28,139	275	2,873,669	23,345
1993	1,511,741	14,821	35,443	350	3,145,544	25,781
1994	1,513,402	14,948	40,786	390	3,395,798	27,356
1995	1,545,584	15,334	43,725	417	3,593,347	28,524
1996	1,559,130	15,213	47,954	428	3,762,107	29,255
1997	1,570,709	14,892	49,166	460	3,891,566	29,369
1998	2,163,161	27,159	70,009	682	4,323,622	39,539

SOURCE: The Bank of Japan.

the BIS capital ratio.[52] By 1998, the guarantee schemes had grown so rapidly (Table 14) that they had nearly exhausted their funding. Late in that year, therefore, the government offered them additional funding of 20 trillion yen. In the summer of 1999, a new round of fund injections was approved, and in September 1999, yet another scheme was announced to guarantee the corporate-bond issues of small and medium-sized companies.

Government lending agencies funded through the postal savings system also increased their lending to small and medium-sized enterprises in 1997.[53] Indeed, it is reported that some banks tried to recover their impaired loans from these companies by asking them to borrow from the government agencies.

The Legal Resolution Framework and Further Recapitalization

The Financial Supervisory Agency (FSA) was established in June 1998 to take over the supervision of banks from the Ministry of Finance and to consolidate the segmented supervisory function previously held by

---

[52] These schemes allow banks to engage in higher-risk lending to boost their margins.

[53] These agencies are primarily providers of housing loans and of long-term loans to small and medium-sized enterprises. They generally offer lower lending rates than banks offer, partly because they are not profit oriented.

various bodies.[54] It was granted considerable operational autonomy and independence so as to allow the supervisors to operate more effectively.

In October 1998, the Diet passed the Financial Revitalization Law and the Financial Early Strengthening Law and amended the Deposit Insurance Law to provide a broad framework for the resolution of banking problems. The new laws augmented existing procedures for dealing with bank failures by introducing management by financial-resolution administrators as well as temporary nationalization or special public management. The new laws also merged the Resolution and Collection Bank and the Housing Loan Administration Corporation into the Resolution and Collection Corporation, the expanded mandate of which allowed it to purchase bad loans not only from failed banks, but also from solvent financial institutions.

At the same time, the Diet doubled the total amount of government funds set aside for the strengthening of the banking sector to 60 trillion yen (12 percent of GDP), out of which 25 trillion yen were earmarked for recapitalizing weak but solvent banks, 18 trillion yen were earmarked for dealing with insolvent banks through nationalization and liquidation, and 17 trillion yen were earmarked for full deposit protection of insolvent banks. The Financial Revitalization Committee (FRC) was established to oversee the bank-restructuring process.

The increased funding allowed for additional capital injections into the banks. By the end of March 1999, bank applications for a second round of government-capital injection asked for 7.5 trillion yen, four times as much as the first round in 1998. The modalities of the injection were the purchases by the Deposit Insurance Corporation of preferred shares and subordinated debts issued by the banks. Contrary to the injection in 1998, the amounts varied by bank and reflected the condition of individual banks. To qualify for capital injection, the FRC required each bank to submit a restructuring plan (including the raising of new capital from the private sector) that would be subject to review on a quarterly basis. If not satisfied with the restructuring progress of a bank, the FSA could convert its holdings of preferred stocks to common stocks after a grace period (the length of the period varies and reflects the strength of the bank) and could, as largest

[54] The FSA took over the supervision of banks, securities firms, insurance companies, and nonbank financial institutions from the Ministry of Finance, the supervision of *shinkin* banks from the Regional Financial Bureaus, and the supervision of credit cooperatives from the prefectural governments.

shareholder, put pressure on the management. The Bank of Tokyo-Mitsubishi, the largest and the soundest bank, did not apply for capital injection. Instead, it made public its intention to pay off the subordinated debt it had issued to the government in March 1998.

These new measures allowed the FSA to tighten the operations of its supervisory authority. After conducting full-scale on-site examinations of sixteen major banks (nine city banks, one long-term-credit bank, six trust banks) in the fall of 1998 and of all regional banks in the winter and spring of 1999, the FSA concluded that the self-assessment of asset quality undertaken by the banks in March 1998 was based on assumptions that were too optimistic and that the banks had significantly understated their nonperforming loans.

Closures or suspensions of banks continued during 1998. The Long Term Credit Bank of Japan, which announced its merger plan with Sumitomo Trust Bank in June 1998, was nationalized in October 1998 after the law for temporary nationalization was passed. Nippon Credit Bank was nationalized later in the year. The net worth of these banks had become negative after the FSA asked them to apply stricter loan-classification standards and to make provisions accordingly. The Deposit Insurance Company acquired all the outstanding shares of both banks and provided financial support to allow them to continue their operations. The government's capital injection to the banks at the end of March 1998, however, proved to be worthless.

Once the FRC and the FSA were satisfied that, after the second round of public-capital injection, the major banks had sufficient capital (with a capital-adequacy ratio of 10 percent or more based on the stricter loan classification), they turned their attention to the regional banks. In April 1999, the FSA extended the PCA framework to banks without international operations.[55]

The FRC also announced guidelines for government injection of capital to regional banks. Public funds would be used either to support banks that were indispensable for the growth of the regional economy

[55] Based on the result of a special inspection, the FSA declared three regional II banks (Kofuku, Kokumin, and Tokyo Sowa) insolvent and placed them under the government's control. The FSA also recommended the merger of Hanshin Bank with Midori Bank. As noted, Midori Bank had been established in August 1995 to take over Hyogo Bank and had since been functioning in western Japan as the American Resolution Trust Corporation functioned in the United States). The FSA also ordered two regional II banks (Namihaya and Niigata-Chuo) and one regional I bank (Hokkaido) to increase their capital to meet the 4 percent capital-adequacy requirement. Kofuku, Kokumin, Tokyo Sowa, Namihaya, and Niigata-Chuo Banks all declared bankruptcy in 1999.

or to facilitate consolidation of banks. The FRC required that banks applying for public funds meet a capital-adequacy standard of 8 percent instead of the 4 percent domestic capital-adequacy requirement.

In September 1999, the FRC approved the application by three regional I banks (Ashikaga, Hokuriku, and Ryukyu) and one regional II bank (Hiroshima Sogou) for capital injections totaling 260 billion yen, after which they met the capital-adequacy ratio of 8 percent.

In 2000, the Deposit Insurance Law was revised to introduce purchase and assumptions procedures to expedite the resolution of troubled banks. These procedures are designed to maximize the value of failed banks by allowing the receivers to resolve separately (and thus more quickly) their good assets. The revision also extends the coverage of deposit insurance to bank debentures and interests.

8   Some Positive Recent Developments

Although it would appear that the Japanese banking crisis has, for the time being, been stabilized, the long-term health of the sector still depends heavily on the ability of the banks to undertake meaningful restructuring. Such restructuring must include tackling the still sizable asset-quality problems, dealing with weak corporate profitability, and strengthening corporate governance. This section discusses several recent developments that, in many respects, depart from old practices. Should these developments become part of a trend, they bode well for the future:

• The new millennium has seen a series of voluntary mergers, the first since a number that occurred during the early 1990s and since the merger between the Bank of Tokyo and Mitsubishi Bank in April 1996.[56] These mergers have led to the consolidation of the major banks into four groups: Mizuho Holdings, Mitsui-Sumitomo Bank, Mitsubishi Tokyo Financial Group, and United Financial of Japan.[57]

---

[56] Mitsui Bank and Taiyo-Kobe Bank merged into Sakura Bank in 1990, and Kyowa Bank and Saitama Bank merged into Asahi Bank in 1991.

[57] Mizuho Holdings, Inc., was formed as a holding company of the Industrial Bank of Japan, Dai-Ichi Kangyo Bank, and Fuji Bank. Mitsui-Sumitomo Bank was formed by a merger between Sumitomo Bank and Sakura Bank. The Mitsubishi Tokyo Financial Group was formed as a holding company of the Bank of Tokyo Mitsubishi, Mitsubishi Trust Bank, and Nippon Trust Bank. The United Financial of Japan was formed as a holding company of Sanwa Bank, Tokai Bank, and Toyo Trust Bank. Chuo-Mitsui Trust Bank (which itself is a result of a merger between Chuo Trust Bank and Mitsui Trust Bank) is expected eventually to join the Mitsui-Sumitomo Bank Group. The major banks

These mergers are significant because they reflect the banks' recognition of the need to reduce overcapacity (through, for example, layoffs and branch consolidation), even when this may require a surrender of power by the management of the individual merging banks. Whether these mergers will eventually lead to the much-needed downsizing and diversification of the banking business, however, is yet to be seen.[58]

• The merger between Sumitomo Bank and Sakura Bank is of particular importance because it joins banks belonging to two competing industrial groups (Sumitomo and Mitsui). The rivalry between industrial groups in Japan has until now prevented such corporate restructuring. To the extent that the merger between Sumitomo and Sakura represents a fracturing of the industrial-group system, it may encourage corporate restructuring between *keiretsu* and create an impetus for economy-wide restructuring in Japan.

• Another positive development was the approval by the FRC, in September 1999, of the application by Ripplewood Holdings (an American investment firm) to acquire the nationalized Long Term Credit Bank of Japan. This is an important milestone, because it was the first time a foreign financial institution acquired a major bank in Japan.[59] The sale of the Long Term Credit Bank (now renamed Shinsei Bank) has opened the Japanese market to foreign competitors. If this trend continues, it will reinforce the introduction of modern banking practices in Japan.

• Although concerns about nonperforming loans continue to persist, the FSA is now actively putting pressure on banks to accelerate the disposal of these loans. The FSA is preparing a new guideline under which banks must write off loans in the "doubtful" and "loss" categories within three years after they have been classified in these categories.[60]

---

remaining outside the four groups are Asahi Bank, Daiwa Bank, Sumitomo Trust Bank (still independent, although closely related to Mitsui-Sumitomo Banking Group) and Norin Chuo Kinko.

[58] Some critics of the planned mergers, while raising questions about whether the mergers are likely to generate real restructuring, have pointed out that they could further undermine the discipline in the system by making banks even bigger, thus accommodating the authorities' "too big to fail" strategy ("A Pitfall in the Consolidation of the Big Banks," 1999).

[59] Merrill Lynch bought Yamaichi Securities in 1998, and since 2000, foreign strategic investors have acquired four insurance companies. In 2001, American Lone Star bought Tokyo Sowa Bank.

[60] Banks will be required to write off loans that have already been classified in these categories within two years after the implementation of the new guidelines.

This guideline is intended to help accelerate corporate restructuring and improve the reallocation of economic resources. In addition, marking-to-market accounting has been introduced for securities in investment accounts in the current fiscal year. The new accounting framework requires banks to deduct 60 percent (assuming a 40 percent effective tax rate) of unrealized loss of their securities holdings from retained earnings.

• There are signs that regulators are now preparing to tackle the issue of the large equity holdings of banks. The government is expected to announce soon a new regulation that will require banks to reduce their equity holdings to no more than their equity capital by 2004. To facilitate the implementation of the new regulation, the government is deliberating a new law that will provide tax incentives to banks that sell their shares to a special institution to be established by the government (but capitalized by banks). Under this plan, the government will provide some guarantee on losses incurred by an institution when it liquidates its shares (banks will be required to absorb part of any loss, with the government picking up the rest). In addition, the FSA is reportedly considering a plan that will place 150 percent risk weight on equity holdings in the calculation of the BIS capital ratio and require banks to use a market-risk model to assess the required capital for shareholdings. These regulations, if implemented, will help reduce the vulnerability of banks to fluctuations in stock prices and diminish incentives for cross-shareholdings (both of which should improve the governance of the corporate sector).

• The new government of Prime Minister Koizumi recently announced that it would consider privatizing governmental agencies with lending or deposit-taking activities (Postal Savings System, Development Bank of Japan, Japan Bank for International Cooperation, and Housing Loan Corporation). Such steps will allow the rationalization of the loan pricing and help strengthen the private banks.

9 Conclusion

Several important lessons can be drawn from the experience of the Japanese banking crisis:

• When market forces do not promote consolidation and the timely exit of unprofitable institutions, deregulation in a financial system already characterized by overcapacity can lead to excessive competition and risk taking, with the consequence that the resilience and health of

45

financial institutions will be weakened (Nishimura, 1999). This is especially true when deregulation is not accompanied by a corresponding adjustment to the regulatory framework and by internal risk-management control.

• Uncoordinated deregulation, such as when the pace of deregulation is uneven across different kinds of financial institutions, can be particularly harmful. "Regulatory arbitrage," resulting from unequal regulatory and supervisory treatments of different financial institutions engaging in similar activities, can give rise to unhealthy competition and concentration of risks. The sequencing of deregulation is also important. The fact that Japanese banks were not allowed to underwrite securities,[61] even while the bond market was being liberalized (which made alternative sources of funding available for blue-chip corporations) probably contributed to the weakening of the banks.

• Property cycles and asset bubbles can have profound repercussions on the health of the financial system; financial deregulation in an expansionary macroeconomic environment may contribute to inflation in asset prices. To mitigate these repercussions, prudent banking requires banks to base their lending decisions on cash-flow analyses of the borrowers (rather than simple collateral requirements) and to adjust their assessment of the creditworthiness of the borrowers in a timely manner. Because economic cycles are difficult to forecast, procyclical provisioning requirements may be useful in protecting banks from unexpected economic downturns.

• The main-bank system, which is centered on the monitoring role of the main banks, relies excessively on the ability of these banks to execute their role effectively. Distressed main banks may not have the proper incentive to relay the true conditions of troubled borrowers to other creditors and to initiate and carry out the necessary restructuring process. They may, instead, delay dealing with the troubled borrowers by exercising forbearance, thereby worsening the problem.

• Weak corporate governance may prevent banks from undertaking meaningful restructuring to arrest their deterioration. Effective corporate governance, which requires shareholder activism and includes disclosure standards, effective internal and external audits, separation between board and management, and the accountability of board directors to shareholders and regulators, is critical in providing the necessary checks and balances among shareholders, bank boards, and

[61] Banks were not allowed to set up securities subsidiaries until 1994.

bank management. Cross-shareholding between banks and their borrowers may, on the one hand, prevent banks from taking forceful action against their troubled borrowers and, on the other, discourage the shareholder-borrowers from playing their role in the corporate governance of the banks.

• Transparent accounting standards (with regard to loan classification, accrual of interest, and marking-to-market of assets) are an important tool in effective supervision. Accounting standards should be designed around the need to promote substance over form and to discourage manipulation. Consolidated accounting, especially when there are substantial transactions between financial institutions and their affiliates and subsidiaries, facilitates consolidated supervision. Inclusion of qualification by accountants should be an integral part of the publicly disclosed audited financial statements.

• Although the regulation and supervision of banks constitute the last line of defense, regulatory authorities need to take a proactive attitude toward supervision. Regulatory forbearance may postpone a crisis, but only at the price of raising the fiscal cost of the final resolution. A Prompt Corrective Action framework is often necessary to force or empower the regulators to take difficult action against weak financial institutions, especially when the problems arise from supervisory negligence.

References

Ammer, John, and Michael Gibson, "Regulation and the Cost of Capital in Japan: A Case Study," International Finance Discussion Paper No. 556, Washington, D.C., Board of Governors of the Federal Reserve System, July 1996.

Ammer, John, Michael Gibson, and Amnon Levy, "Underpriced Again: The April 1996 Tokai Bank Euro-Convertible Preference Issue," Washington, D.C., Board of Governors of the Federal Reserve System, May 1996, processed.

Aoki, Masahiko, and Hugh Patrick, The Japanese Main Bank System: Its Relevance for Developing and Transforming Economies, Oxford and New York, Oxford University Press, 1994.

Bank of Japan, Quarterly Bulletin, November 1996.

———, "Comparative Economic and Financial Statistics—Japan and Other Major Countries," Tokyo, Bank of Japan, 1999, processed.

Bayoumi, Tamim, "The Morning After: Explaining the Slowdown in Japanese Growth in the 1990s," International Monetary Fund Working Paper No. 99/13, Washington, D.C., International Monetary Fund, January 1999.

Brunner Allan, and Steven Kamin, "Bank Lending and Economic Activity in Japan: Did 'Financial Factors' Contribute to the Recent Downturn?" *International Journal of Finance and Economics*, 3 (January 1998), pp. 73–89.

Cargill, Thomas, "What Caused Japan's Banking Crisis?" in Takeo Hoshi and Hugh Patrick, eds., *Crisis and Change in the Japanese Financial System*, Dordrecht, Boston, and New York, Kluwer, 2000, pp. 37–58.

Cargill, Thomas, Michael Hutchison, and Takatoshi Ito, "Preventing Future Banking Crisis in Japan," paper prepared for the Federal Reserve Bank of Chicago and World Bank Conference on Preventing Banking Crisis: Analysis and Lessons from Recent Bank Failures, Chicago, June 11–13, 1997.

Corbett, Jenny, "Crisis, What Crisis? The Policy Response to Japan's Banking Crisis," in Craig Freedman, ed., *Why did Japan Stumble? Causes and Cures*, Cheltenham and Northampton, Edward Elgar, 2000a, pp. 191–224.

———, "Japan's Banking Crisis in International Perspective," in Masahiko Aoki and Gary Saxonhouse, eds., *Finance, Governance and Competitiveness in Japan*, Oxford and New York, Oxford University Press, 2000b, pp. 139–176.

Cortavarria, Luis, Claudia Dziobek, Akihiro Kanaya, and Inwon Song, "Loan Review, Provisioning, and Macroeconomic Linkages," in Charles Enoch, David Marston, and Michael Taylor, eds., *Building Strong Banks: Surveillance and Resolution*, Washington, D.C., International Monetary Fund, forthcoming 2001.

Federation of Bankers Association of Japan, "The Banking System in Japan," Tokyo, Federation of Bankers Association of Japan, 1989.

Fukao, Mitsuhiro, "Japanese Financial Instability and Weaknesses in the Corporate Governance Structure," *Seoul Journal of Economics*, 11 (Winter 1988), pp. 381–422.

Fukuda, Atsuo, and Shin'ichi Hirota, "Main Bank Relationships and Capital Structure in Japan," *Journal of the Japanese and International Economies*, 10 (September 1996), pp. 250–161.

Genay, Hesna, "The Ownership Structure of Japanese Financial Institutions," Academic Working Paper Series No. 93–19, Chicago, Federal Reserve Bank of Chicago, January 1993.

Gray, Simon, and David Woo, "Reconsidering External Financing of Domestic Budget Deficits—Debunking Some Received Wisdom," Policy Discussion Paper No. 00/8, Washington D.C., International Monetary Fund, July 2000.

Hoshi, Takeo, and Anil Kashyap, "The Japanese Banking Crisis: Where Did It Come From and How Will It End," National Bureau of Economic Research Working Paper No. 7250, Cambridge, Mass., National Bureau of Economic Research, July 1999.

Hsu, Robert, *The MIT Dictionary of the Japanese Economy*, Cambridge, Mass., MIT Press, 1994.

Hutchinson, Michael, and Kathleen McDill, "Are All Banking Crises Alike? The Japanese Experience in International Comparison," National Bureau of Economic Research Working Paper No. 7253, Cambridge, Mass., National Bureau of Economic Research, July 1999.

Irvine, Steven, "Why Japanese Banks Don't Care About Profits," *Euromoney*, February 1998, pp. 66–70.

Kawai, Masahiro, Juro Hashimoto, and Shigemi Izumida, "Japanese Firms in Financial Distress and Main Banks: Analyses of Interest-Rate Premia," *Japan and the World Economy*, 8 (No. 2, 1996), pp. 175–194.

Levy, Joaquim, "Resolving Japan's Banking System Problems," in *Japan: Selected Issues*, Washington, D.C., International Monetary Fund, October 1998, pp. 101–125.

Marsh, Terry, and Jean-Michel Paul, "Japanese Banks' Bad Loans: What Happened," Department of Economics, University of California at Berkeley, 1996, processed.

Morsink, James, and Tamim Bayoumi, "A Peek Inside the Black Box: The Monetary Transmission Mechanism in Japan," International Monetary Fund Working Paper No. 99/137, Washington, D.C., International Monetary Fund, October 1999.

Motonishi, Taizo, and Hiroshi Yoshikawa, "Causes of the Long Stagnation of Japan During the 1990s: Financial or Real?" National Bureau of Economic Research Working Paper No. 7351, Cambridge, Mass., National Bureau of Economic Research, September 1999.

Nishimura, Yoshimasa "Causes of the Failures of the Supervision over Financial Institutions" (in Japanese), Bungeishunju, Bunshun Bunko, 1999.

Noma, Toshikatsu, "Scale-Maximizing Behavior of the Japanese Banks: An Empirical Analysis" (in Japanese, with English summary), *Economic Studies Quarterly*, 37 (December 1986), pp. 336–350.

"A Pitfall in the Consolidation of the Big Banks," *Nikkei*, December 8, 1999.

Sekine, Toshitaka, "Firm Investment and Balance-Sheet Problems in Japan," International Monetary Fund Working Paper No. 99/111, Washington, D.C., International Monetary Fund, August 1999.

Sundararajan, V., and Tomás Baliño, "Issues in Recent Banking Crises," in Sundararajan and Baliño, eds., *Banking Crises: Cases and Issues*, Washington, D.C., International Monetary Fund, 1991, pp. 1–57.

Taniuchi, Mitsuru, "Recent Developments in Japan's Financial Sector: Bad Loans and Financial Deregulation," *Journal of Asian Economics*, 8 (Summer, 1997), pp. 225–244.

Woo, David, "In Search of 'Capital Crunch': Supply Factors Behind the Slowdown in Japan," International Monetary Fund Working Paper No. 99/03, Washington, D.C., International Monetary Fund, January 1999.

———, "Two Approaches to Resolving Nonperforming Assets During Financial Crises," in Charles Enoch, David Marston, and Michael Taylor, eds., *Building Strong Banks: Surveillance and Resolution*, Washington, D.C., International Monetary Fund, forthcoming 2001.

Yamaguchi, Yutaka, "Asset Price and Monetary Policy: Japan's Experience," paper presented at the Federal Reserve Bank of Kansas City Symposium on New Challenges for Economic Policy, Jackson Hole, Wyo., August 26–28, 1999.

PUBLICATIONS OF THE
INTERNATIONAL ECONOMICS SECTION

Notice to Contributors

The International Economics Section publishes papers in two series. ESSAYS IN INTERNATIONAL ECONOMICS and PRINCETON STUDIES IN INTERNATIONAL ECONOMICS. Two earlier series, REPRINTS IN INTERNATIONAL FINANCE and SPECIAL PAPERS IN INTERNATIONAL ECONOMICS, have been discontinued, with the SPECIAL PAPERS being absorbed into the STUDIES series.

The Section welcomes the submission of manuscripts focused on topics in international trade, international macroeconomics, or international finance. Submissions should address systemic issues for the global economy or, if concentrating on particular economies, should adopt a comparative perspective.

ESSAYS IN INTERNATIONAL ECONOMICS are meant to disseminate new views about international economic events and policy issues. They should be accessible to a broad audience of professional economists.

PRINCETON STUDIES IN INTERNATIONAL ECONOMICS are devoted to new research in international economics or to synthetic treatments of a body of literature. They should be comparable in originality and technical proficiency to papers published in leading economic journals. Papers that are longer and more complete than those publishable in the professional journals are welcome.

Manuscripts should be submitted in triplicate, typed single sided and double spaced throughout on 8½ by 11 white bond paper. Publication can be expedited if manuscripts are computer keyboarded in WordPerfect or a compatible program. Additional instructions and a style guide are available from the Section or on the website at www.princeton.edu/~ies.

How to Obtain Publications

The Section's publications are distributed free of charge to college, university, and public libraries and to nongovernmental, nonprofit research institutions. Eligible institutions may ask to be placed on the Section's permanent mailing list.

Individuals and institutions not qualifying for free distribution may receive all publications for the calendar year for a subscription fee of $45.00. Late subscribers will receive all back issues for the year during which they subscribe.

Publications may be ordered individually, with payment made in advance. All publications (ESSAYS, STUDIES, SPECIAL PAPERS, and REPRINTS) cost $10.00 each; an additional $1.50 should be sent for postage and handling within the United States, Canada, and Mexico; $4 should be added for surface delivery outside the region.

All payments must be made in U.S. dollars. Subscription fees and charges for single issues will be waived for organizations and individuals in countries where foreign-exchange regulations prohibit dollar payments.

Information about the Section and its publishing program is available on the Section's website at www.princeton.edu/~ies. A subscription and order form is printed at the end of this volume. Correspondence should be addressed to:

International Economics Section
Department of Economics, Fisher Hall
Princeton University
Princeton, New Jersey 08544-1021
Tel: 609-258-4048 • Fax: 609-258-1374
E-mail: ies@princeton.edu

51

List of Recent Publications

A complete list of publications is available at the International Economics Section website at www.princeton.edu/~ies.

ESSAYS IN INTERNATIONAL ECONOMICS
(formerly Essays in International Finance)

183. Michael Bruno, *High Inflation and the Nominal Anchors of an Open Economy.* (June 1991)
184. Jacques J. Polak, *The Changing Nature of IMF Conditionality.* (September 1991)
185. Ethan B. Kapstein, *Supervising International Banks: Origins and Implications of the Basle Accord.* (December 1991)
186. Alessandro Giustiniani, Francesco Papadia, and Daniela Porciani, *Growth and Catch-Up in Central and Eastern Europe: Macroeconomic Effects on Western Countries.* (April 1992)
187. Michele Fratianni, Jürgen von Hagen, and Christopher Waller, *The Maastricht Way to EMU.* (June 1992)
188. Pierre-Richard Agénor, *Parallel Currency Markets in Developing Countries: Theory, Evidence, and Policy Implications.* (November 1992)
189. Beatriz Armendariz de Aghion and John Williamson, *The G-7's Joint-and-Several Blunder.* (April 1993)
190. Paul Krugman, *What Do We Need to Know about the International Monetary System?* (July 1993)
191. Peter M. Garber and Michael G. Spencer, *The Dissolution of the Austro-Hungarian Empire: Lessons for Currency Reform.* (February 1994)
192. Raymond F. Mikesell, *The Bretton Woods Debates: A Memoir.* (March 1994)
193. Graham Bird, *Economic Assistance to Low-Income Countries: Should the Link be Resurrected?* (July 1994)
194. Lorenzo Bini-Smaghi, Tommaso Padoa-Schioppa, and Francesco Papadia, *The Transition to EMU in the Maastricht Treaty.* (November 1994)
195. Ariel Buira, *Reflections on the International Monetary System.* (January 1995)
196. Shinji Takagi, *From Recipient to Donor: Japan's Official Aid Flows, 1945 to 1990 and Beyond.* (March 1995)
197. Patrick Conway, *Currency Proliferation: The Monetary Legacy of the Soviet Union.* (June 1995)
198. Barry Eichengreen, *A More Perfect Union? The Logic of Economic Integration.* (June 1996)
199. Peter B. Kenen, ed., with John Arrowsmith, Paul De Grauwe, Charles A. E. Goodhart, Daniel Gros, Luigi Spaventa, and Niels Thygesen, *Making EMU Happen—Problems and Proposals: A Symposium.* (August 1996)
200. Peter B. Kenen, ed., with Lawrence H. Summers, William R. Cline, Barry Eichengreen, Richard Portes, Arminio Fraga, and Morris Goldstein, *From Halifax to Lyons: What Has Been Done about Crisis Management?* (October 1996)
201. Louis W. Pauly, *The League of Nations and the Foreshadowing of the International Monetary Fund.* (December 1996)

202. Harold James, *Monetary and Fiscal Unification in Nineteenth-Century Germany: What Can Kohl Learn from Bismarck?* (March 1997)
203. Andrew Crockett, *The Theory and Practice of Financial Stability.* (April 1997)
204. Benjamin J. Cohen, *The Financial Support Fund of the OECD: A Failed Initiative.* (June 1997)
205. Robert N. McCauley, *The Euro and the Dollar.* (November 1997)
206. Thomas Laubach and Adam S. Posen, *Disciplined Discretion: Monetary Targeting in Germany and Switzerland.* (December 1997)
207. Stanley Fischer, Richard N. Cooper, Rudiger Dornbusch, Peter M. Garber, Carlos Massad, Jacques J. Polak, Dani Rodrik, and Savak S. Tarapore, *Should the IMF Pursue Capital-Account Convertibility?* (May 1998)
208. Charles P. Kindleberger, *Economic and Financial Crises and Transformations in Sixteenth-Century Europe.* (June 1998)
209. Maurice Obstfeld, *EMU: Ready or Not?* (July 1998)
210. Wilfred Ethier, *The International Commercial System.* (September 1998)
211. John Williamson and Molly Mahar, *A Survey of Financial Liberalization.* (November 1998)
212. Ariel Buira, *An Alternative Approach to Financial Crises.* (February 1999)
213. Barry Eichengreen, Paul Masson, Miguel Savastano, and Sunil Sharma, *Transition Strategies and Nominal Anchors on the Road to Greater Exchange-Rate Flexibility.* (April 1999)
214. Curzio Giannini, *"Enemy of None but a Common Friend of All"? An International Perspective on the Lender-of-Last-Resort Function.* (June 1999)
215. Jeffrey A. Frankel, *No Single Currency Regime Is Right for All Countries or at All Times.* (August 1999)
216. Jacques J. Polak, *Streamlining the Financial Structure of the International Monetary Fund.* (September 1999)
217. Gustavo H. B. Franco, *The Real Plan and the Exchange Rate.* (April 2000)
218. Thomas D. Willett, *International Financial Markets as Sources of Crises or Discipline: The Too Much, Too Late Hypothesis.* (May 2000)
219. Richard H. Clarida, *G-3 Exchange-Rate Relationships: A Review of the Record and of Proposals for Change.* (September 2000)
220. Stanley Fischer, *On the Need for an International Lender of Last Resort.* (November 2000)
221. Benjamin J. Cohen, *Life at the Top: International Currencies in the Twenty-First Century.* (December 2000)
222. Akihiro Kanaya and David Woo, *The Japanese Banking Crisis of the 1990s: Sources and Lessons.* (June 2001)

PRINCETON STUDIES IN INTERNATIONAL ECONOMICS
(formerly Princeton Studies in International Finance)

71. Daniel Gros and Alfred Steinherr, *Economic Reform in the Soviet Union: Pas de Deux between Disintegration and Macroeconomic Destabilization.* (November 1991)
72. George M. von Furstenberg and Joseph P. Daniels, *Economic Summit Declarations, 1975-1989: Examining the Written Record of International Cooperation.* (February 1992)

73. Ishac Diwan and Dani Rodrik, *External Debt, Adjustment, and Burden Sharing: A Unified Framework*. (November 1992)
74. Barry Eichengreen, *Should the Maastricht Treaty Be Saved?* (December 1992)
75. Adam Klug, *The German Buybacks, 1932-1939: A Cure for Overhang?* (November 1993)
76. Tamim Bayoumi and Barry Eichengreen, *One Money or Many? Analyzing the Prospects for Monetary Unification in Various Parts of the World.* (September 1994)
77. Edward E. Leamer, *The Heckscher-Ohlin Model in Theory and Practice.* (February 1995)
78. Thorvaldur Gylfason, *The Macroeconomics of European Agriculture.* (May 1995)
79. Angus S. Deaton and Ronald I. Miller, *International Commodity Prices, Macroeconomic Performance, and Politics in Sub-Saharan Africa.* (December 1995)
80. Chander Kant, *Foreign Direct Investment and Capital Flight.* (April 1996)
81. Gian Maria Milesi-Ferretti and Assaf Razin, *Current-Account Sustainability.* (October 1996)
82. Pierre-Richard Agénor, *Capital-Market Imperfections and the Macroeconomic Dynamics of Small Indebted Economies.* (June 1997)
83. Michael Bowe and James W. Dean, *Has the Market Solved the Sovereign-Debt Crisis?* (August 1997)
84. Willem H. Buiter, Giancarlo M. Corsetti, and Paolo A. Pesenti, *Interpreting the ERM Crisis: Country-Specific and Systemic Issues.* (March 1998)
85. Holger C. Wolf, *Transition Strategies: Choices and Outcomes.* (June 1999)
86. Alessandro Prati and Garry J. Schinasi, *Financial Stability in European Economic and Monetary Union.* (August 1999)
87. Peter Hooper, Karen Johnson, and Jaime Marquez, *Trade Elasticities for the G-7 Countries.* (August 2000)
88. Ramkishen S. Rajan, *(Ir)relevance of Currency-Crisis Theory to the Devaluation and Collapse of the Thai Baht.* (February 2001)
89. Lucio Sarno and Mark P. Taylor, *The Microstructure of the Foreign-Exchange Market: A Selective Survey of the Literature.* (May 2001)

SPECIAL PAPERS IN INTERNATIONAL ECONOMICS

16. Elhanan Helpman, *Monopolistic Competition in Trade Theory.* (June 1990)
17. Richard Pomfret, *International Trade Policy with Imperfect Competition.* (August 1992)
18. Hali J. Edison, *The Effectiveness of Central-Bank Intervention: A Survey of the Literature After 1982.* (July 1993)
19. Sylvester W.C. Eijffinger and Jakob De Haan, *The Political Economy of Central-Bank Independence.* (May 1996)
20. Olivier Jeanne, *Currency Crises: A Perspective on Recent Theoretical Developments.* (March 2000)

REPRINTS IN INTERNATIONAL FINANCE

29. Peter B. Kenen, *Sorting Out Some EMU Issues*; reprinted from Jean Monnet Chair Paper 38, Robert Schuman Centre, European University Institute, 1996. (December 1996)

○ SUBSCRIBE ○ ORDER ○

INTERNATIONAL ECONOMICS SECTION

SUBSCRIPTIONS

Rate $45 a year

The International Economics Section issues six to eight publications each year in a mix of Essays and Studies. Late subscribers receive all publications for the subscription year. Prepayment is required and may be made by check in U.S. dollars or by Visa or MasterCard. A complete list of publications (including previously issued Special Papers and Reprints) is available at www.princeton.edu/~ies.

Address inquiries to:

International Economics Section
Department of Economics, Fisher Hall
Princeton University
Princeton, NJ 08544–1021

BOOK ORDERS

Essays, Studies, Special Papers
& Reprints $10.00

plus postage

Within U.S. $1.50
Outside U.S. (surface mail) $4.00

_____

Discounts are available for orders of five or more publications.

_____

Telephone: 609–258–4048
Telefax: 609–258–1374
E-mail: ies@princeton.edu

fold up

INTERNATIONAL ECONOMICS SECTION

This is a subscription ☐ ; a book order ☐

Essay #(s) ____, ____ No. of copies___

Study #(s) ____, ____ No. of copies___

Special Paper # ____   No. of copies ___

Reprint # ____   No. of copies ___

☐ Enclosed is my check made payable to Princeton University, International Economics Section

totaling $_____.

Please charge: ☐ Visa ☐ MasterCard

Acct.# _____

Expires _____

Signature_____

Send to:

Name_____

Address_____

City _____

State _____Zip _____

Country_____

INTERNATIONAL ECONOMICS SECTION
DEPARTMENT OF ECONOMICS
FISHER HALL
PRINCETON UNIVERSITY
PRINCETON, NJ 08544-1021